Āditya Hṛdayam

।। आदित्य हृदयम् ।।

Rediscovering Indian Literary Classics
(ISSN - 0972-0111)

1. Taittirīya Upaniṣad: With the Original Text in Sanskrit and Roman Transliteration. Translation with an Exhaustive Commentary; by Muni Narayana Prasad. (ISBN 81-246-0014-7)

2,4-5. Bṛhadāraṇyaka Upaniṣad: With Original Text in Roman Transliteration. English Translation and Appendices; by Nitya Chaitanya Yati; Vol. 1: Madhu Kāṇḍa; Vol. 2: Muni Kāṇḍa; Vol. 3: Khila Kāṇḍa. (ISBN 81-246-0008-2)

3. Kena Upaniṣad: With the Original Text in Sanskrit and Roman Transliteration. Translation with an Extensive Commentary; by Muni Narayana Prasad. (ISBN 81-246-0034-1)

6. Muṇḍaka Upaniṣad: With the Original Text in Sanskrit and Roman Transliteration. Translation with an Exhaustive Commentary; by Muni Narayana Prasad. (ISBN 81-246-0105-4)

7. Kaṭha Upaniṣad: With the Original Text in Sanskrit and Roman transliteration. Translation with an Exhaustive Commentary; by Muni Narayana Prasad. (ISBN 81-246-0110-0)

8. Praśna Upaniṣad: With the Original Text in Sanskrit and Roman transliteration. Translation with an Extensive Commentary; by Muni Narayana Prasad. (ISBN 81-246-0129-1)

9. Aitareya Upaniṣad: With the Original Text in Sanskrit and Roman transliteration. Translation with an Extensive Commentary; by Muni Narayana Prasad. (ISBN 81-246-0142-9)

10. Śrī Dakṣiṇāmūrti Stotram of Śrī Śaṅkarācārya; with the commentary Tattvaprakāśikā; by Swami Tattvavidananda Saraswati; Edited by Puppala B. (ISBN 81-246-0210-7)

12. Vāstuśāstra: Ancient Indian Architecture and Civil Engineering — Retrospects and Prospects; by Rahul Kumar Altekar (ISBN 978-81-246-0246-1)

13. Gaṇapati Upaniṣad: With the Commentary Tattvaprakāśikā; by Swami Tattvavidananda Saraswati (ISBN 978-81-246-0265-2)

14. Life's Pilgrimage Through the Gītā; by Swami Muni Narayana Prasad (ISBN 978-81-246-0310-9)

15. Chāndogya Upaniṣad; by Swami Muni Narayana Prasad (ISBN 978-81-246-0374-1)

16. Īśavāsya and Māṇḍūkya Upaniṣad; by Swami Muni Narayana Prasad (ISBN 978-81-246-0492-2)

17. Reconstructing Devotion Through Nārada Bhakti Sūtra; by Alka Tyagi (ISBN 978-81-246-0954-5)

Rediscovering Indian Literary Classics, no. 11

Āditya Hṛdayam

with the Commentary *Tattvaprakāśikā*

।। आदित्य हृदयम् ।।

। तत्त्वप्रकाशिका समेतम् ।

by

Swami Tattvavidananda Saraswati

DK PRINTWORLD®
Publishers of Indian Traditions

Cataloging in Publication Data — DK
[Courtesy: D.K. Agencies (P) Ltd. <docinfo@dkagencies.com>]

Vālmīki, author.
Āditya hr̥dayam : with the commentary Tattvaprakāśikā = Āditya hr̥dayam : Tattvaprakāśikā sametam / [edited] by Swami Tattvavidananda Saraswati. – Seventh impression.
pages cm. – (Rediscovering Indian literary classics, ISSN 0972-0111 ; no. 11)
English and Sanskrit (Sanskrit in Latin and Devanagari).
"First published in India in 2003" – Title page verso.
Includes index.
ISBN 9788124602317 (PB)

1. Surya (Hindu deity) – Prayers and devotions. I. Tattvavidananda Saraswati, Swami, 1948- editor. II. Vālmīki Rāmāyaṇa Ādityahr̥dayastotra. III. Vālmīki. Rāmāyaṇa Ādityahr̥dayastotra. English. IV. Tattvavidananda Saraswati, Swami, 1948- Tattvaprakāśikā. V. Title. VI. Series: Rediscovering Indian literary classics ; no. 11.

LCC BL1139.242.A35E5 2025 | DDC 294.5922 23

ISBN: 978-81-246-0231-7 (Pb)
First published in India in 2003
Reprinted, 2004, 2007, 2011, 2017, 2020
Seventh impression, 2025

Printed and published by:
D.K. Printworld (P) Ltd.
Regd. Office: Vedaśrī, F-395, Sudarshan Park
(Metro Station: ESI Hospital), New Delhi – 110015
Phones: (011) 4172 2626, 98713 94815
e-mail: indology@dkprintworld.com
Website: www.dkprintworld.com

Foreword

VIJAYALAKSHMI and I discovered the Arsha Vidya Gurukulam in the fall of 1991. Someone told us about a temple in Saylorsburg, PA, not too far away from our home in New Jersey. We drove up to the Gurukulam and were fortunate to listen to Pujya Swami Dayananda Saraswati, teaching a Vedānta class. Growing up in south India, *sannyāsī* was a familiar part of our environment but we did not have much knowledge of Vedānta. Since that fortuitous fall weekend of 1991, we have been systematically exposed to the teachings of our ancient sages through Pujya Swami Dayananda Saraswati and other teachers at the Gurukulam. It is the collective destiny of all of us living in the US, and the tri-state area in particular, that we have been blessed with such a teaching institution. Many of us have benefited immensely from the wealth of wisdom offered by the teachers of the Gurukulam.

Pujya Swami Tattvavidanada Saraswati started teaching in the Gurukulam in the fall of 1998. He has been a long-time student of Pujya Swami Dayananda Saraswati and has been teaching Vedānta in India for a number of years. The two most striking things about Swamiji are his clarity of thought and his wealth of knowledge. Swamiji hails from a family of Vedāntic and Vedic scholars and is a great scholar himself. He has a Ph.D. in Chemistry and worked as a scientist in India. He also has a Ph.D. in Sanskrit. He is a walking encyclopedia of Vedānta, the Vedas and the Purāṇas. Like Pujya Swami Dayananda he uses simple and easy-to-understand words to impart complex concepts to the modern mind.

Many devotees like me chant *mantra*s like *Āditya Hṛdayam* without fully understanding their meaning or significance. So it was fitting that Pujya Swamiji unfolded its meaning at the request of our friends, Srimathi and Raghu Iyer. Swamiji has subsequently unfolded the hymns such as *Medhā Sūktam, Gaṇapati Upaniṣat,* etc. These enlightening teachings are in addition to his delightful lectures on *Śrīmadbhāgavatam, Śrīmadrāmāyaṇam,* etc.

This book is based on Pujya Swami Tattvavidananda's talks on *Āditya Hṛdayam*. Given their appeal to seekers in US and other parts of the world, the talks were transcribed. Pujya Swamiji has thoroughly revised the text and incorporated the transliteration and word-to-word meanings. He has also compiled the *Nāmāvalī.*

Sri Puppala B., Brahmavidya Kutir, Secunderabad, India, and Sri Mohan Bhujle, Holmdel, NJ provided excellent editorial assistance. We and Swamiji would like to profusely thank them for their invaluable assistance.

We hope that this book will be of immense help to the seekers chanting this popular *stotra,* and inspire many others who are not exposed to it. We pray that this book will help all seekers in realising the only purpose of life, that of gaining Self-knowledge, which is the ultimate purpose of these *upāsanā*s.

Krishna Kumar (KK) S. Davey **Livingston, N. J.**
October 15, (Vijaya Daśamī), 2002

Contents

Dedicated to my parents
Smt. Rani Seethamma
and
Brahmasri Rani Narasimha Sastry

Introduction

ओम्, रामाय रामभद्राय रामचन्द्राय वेधसे ।
रघुनाथाय नाथाय सीतायाः पतये नमः ।।

कूजन्तं राम रामेति मधुरं मधुराक्षरम् ।
आरुह्य कविताशाखां वन्दे वाल्मीकिकोकिलम् ।।

om, rāmāya rāmabhadrāya rāmacandrāya vedhase ।
raghunāthāya nāthāya sītāyāḥ pataye namaḥ ॥

kūjantaṁ rāma rāmoti madhuraṁ madhurākṣaram ।
āruhya kavitāśākhāṁ vande vālmīkikokilam ॥

THE text *Āditya Hṛdayam* is a part of the immortal epic *Śrīmadrāmāyaṇam* authored by Ādikavi Vālmīki. In the Vedic culture, worshipping of *Īśvara* — *īśvaropāsanā* — is very characteristic and unique, and probably slightly different from what we come across today in the Hindu society. Here, *Īśvara* is worshipped in a form, which is readily available for our perception as part of the Nature before us. For example, *Īśvara* is worshipped as the Fire. The *Ṛgveda*, the foremost of the Vedas, starts with the invocation:

अग्निमीडे पुरोहितम् ।
agnimīḍe purohitam ।
I praise the glory of Agni, who is the foremost as a benefactor.

Here Agni is *Īśvara*. Aurobindo explained the word Agni as the Divine Will and Wisdom. In the Vedic culture, fire is universally taken as the symbol of *Īśvara*. We relate to, or we worship *Īśvara* in the form of fire. Another such altar described in the Vedas is the Sun.

Vedic people regularly practise a particular mode of worship called *sandhyā-vandanā*. It is the most well-known mode of worship in the Vedic culture even today.

Vandanā is *upāsanā* or worship. *Sandhyā* means the junction between the night and day when the Sun rises, or between day and night when the Sun sets. Vaidikas worship *Īśvara* at that time in the form of the Sun. They offer water (*arghya*) thrice to the rising and setting Sun, and then meditate upon *Īśvara* as the presiding deity of the solar orb by reciting the famous Gāyatrī *mantra*.

Gāyatrī is the name of a meter. In the *Gītā* (10-35), *Bhagavān* says:

> गायत्री च्छन्दसामहम् ।
> *gāyatrī cchandasāmaham* ।
> I am the meter *gāyatrī* among the meters.

The meter *gāyatrī* has three lines of eight syllables each. Thus, it has twenty-four syllables in all. Every *mantra* describes the glory of a *devatā*. *Devatā* means a particular manifestation of that *para-Brahman* (or *Īśvara*). Thus, the recitation of a given *mantra* amounts to the worship of *Īśvara* in the manifestation of that particular *devatā*. The *devatā* of the Gāyatrī *mantra* is the Sun.

> तत्सवितुर्वरेण्यं भर्गो देवस्य धीमहि ।
> धियो यो नः प्रचोयदयात् ।।
>
> *tatsaviturvareṇyaṁ bhargo devasya dhīmahi* ।
> *dhiyo yo naḥ pracodayāt* ॥
>
> We meditate upon that supreme light (awareness) of the Lord who creates and nourishes this universe. That Lord alone illuminates and inspires our thoughts.

Para-Brahman is essentially without any form or shape, because intrinsically it is not possible for the Supreme Reality to have a given form or shape. If *Brahman* were to have a given form, then It would become yet one more form subject to the limitations of time and space, and hence unreal. If *Īśvara* were to have a given form, however exalted that form may be, it would be limited in space and time. Space and time are always together. Whatever is limited in space is necessarily limited in time. *Īśvara*, who is the originator of space and time, cannot be really folded into space and time. Therefore, *Īśvara* is the attributeless infinite Awareness. *Bhargaḥ* means that *caitanya*, Awareness. It is the origin of the *kriyā-śakti* (energy, potential or expressed in the form of action) and *jñāna-śakti* (the power of knowledge). This entire universe is nothing but a combination of *kriyā-śakti* and *jñāna-śakti*. All the matter comes under the category of *kriyā-śakti* alone. *Bhargaḥ*, the Awareness is the origin of these two. *Bhargaḥ*, the *caitanya* which is *para-Brahman* is called *tat*, *tat bhargaḥ*. *Tat* is *sarvanāma*, a pronoun. The word *sarvanāma* means the name of everything. Everything is a manifestation of *para-Brahman*. Hence, the name of everything also represents the origin of everything. Worship of the *para-Brahman* in a given altar is called *saguṇa* (*sākāra*) *upāsanā*. *Saguṇa* means having attributes; *sākāra* means having a particular form. There is a problem in worshipping the *para-Brahman* in Its attributeless formless nature. *Bhagavān* says in the *Gītā* (12-5):

> क्लेशोऽधिकतरस्तेषामव्यक्तासक्तचेतसाम् ।
> अव्यक्ता हि गतिर्दुःखं देहवद्भिरवाप्यते ।।
>
> *kleśo'dhikatarasteṣāmavyaktāsaktacetasām* ।
> *avyaktā hi gatirduḥkhaṁ dehavadbhiravāpyate* ।।
>
> The affliction is greater still for those whose minds are committed to what cannot be objectified, because an end which cannot be objectified is reached with difficulty by those who are identified with the body.

For a limited being (*jīva*) rooted to the body, identified with the body, appreciation of formless attributeless *para-Brahman* straightaway is a very hard task, for the mind is accustomed to dwell upon names, attributes, and forms. Therefore, *Bhagavān* advises that the devotees may start with the worship or meditation of the *saguṇa*. *Saguṇa* meditation is also called as *apara-Brahma upāsanā*, in contrast to *para-*

Brahma jñāna (knowledge of *para-Brahman*). So, to make meditation easy by taking to an altar of worship, *saguṇa sākāra* has to be superimposed on the attributeless *para-Brahman*. This idea is summarised in the statement:

न ते रूपं न चाकारो नायुधानि न चास्पदम् ।
उपासकानां कार्यार्थं ब्रह्मणो रूपकल्पना ।।

na te rūpaṁ na cākāro nāyudhāni na cāspadam ।
upāsakānāṁ kāryārthaṁ brahmaṇo rūpakalpanā ॥

O Lord, You do not have fixed attributes or form. You do not really wield any weapons. There is no location for you. Yet, for the benefit of meditation upon You by the devotees, a particular form is superimposed on the attributeless *Brahman*.

Meditation on the *saguṇa* helps the seeker to purify the mind and thereby gain a higher level of understanding of the *para-Brahman*.

In the Gāyatrī *mantra*, the Sun god is introduced as *savitur devasya*. This word Savitā appears in the *Āditya Hṛdayam* also. *Īsvara* is called Savitā because he creates, protects and sustains the entire life in this universe. For this reason, the Gāyatrī *mantra* is also called Sāvitrī. With reference to meter it is *gāyatrī*, and with reference to *devatā* it is Sāvitrī. There is one more point of interest in Gāyatrī in the context of *Śrīmadrāmāyaṇam*. If we divide this great epic of 24,000 verses into 24 units of 1000 verses each, then each unit starts with a successive syllable of Gāyatrī. This incorporation of Gāyatrī in the verses of *Śrīmadrāmāyaṇam* makes the latter particularly auspicious. Quite often people ask me a question: Swamiji, can women recite Gāyatrī *mantra*? I quote a verse from *Yama-Smṛti* as the answer to that question.

पुरा कल्पे तु नारीणां मौञ्जीबन्धनमिष्यते ।
अध्यापनं च वेदानां सावित्रीवचनं तथा ।।

purā kalpe tu nārīṇāṁ mauñjībandhanamiṣyate ।
adhyāpanaṁ ca vedānāṁ sāvitrīvacanaṁ tathā ॥

> In the earlier times, the investiture with the sacred thread, teaching of Vedas and recitation of the Gāyatrī was allowed (desired) for the women.

Sītādevī was described by Vālmīki as performing the *sandhyā* meditation in the Aśoka forest, where she was held captive by Rāvaṇa. One should relate to *Īśvara* every morning at the time of sunrise, irrespective of the situation in which one finds oneself, whether one is in prosperity or in adversity. This daily worship called *sandhyā-vandanā* should not be dispensed with.

The Cosmic Person (*Īśvara*), who brought out this universe out of Himself, is often called in the Vedic literature by the name Hiraṇyagarbha from the standpoint of the Universal Power and Omniscience. In the Purāṇic literature, *Īśvara* is referred to as Viṣṇu (one who pervades all) or as Śiva (the auspicious). That Hiraṇyagarbha is worshipped in the altar of the Sun, because, in this Solar system where we live, it is the Sun that is the source of all energy, all activities and all life. That *Īśvara,* who is manifest in the form of the Sun before us, is also present in us in the form of *ātman,* the Awareness, thereby illuminating our thoughts, and making all varieties of knowing possible. If that awareness were not to manifest, then there would have been no faculty of thinking. The power of thinking (*dhī śakti*) is the basis of human existence. A human being is nothing but his ideas and understanding (*buddhi*). The difference between a person in coma and a normal person is the power of thinking alone. In fact, all the metabolic processes such as regulation of body temperature, heartbeat, etc., go on even for a comatose person. The only difference is that his intellect is not functioning. That is also the reason why he is not moving or doing anything. We think that the *buddhi* is present inside the body. But that is wrong. The body exists in the *buddhi*, and that *buddhi* exists in *ātman*, the Awareness, which is that *para-Brahman*. That Awareness (*caitanya*) manifesting in this body-mind-sense complex in the form of consciousness, inspiring the *buddhi-vṛtti*s, is also present before us in the form of the solar orb, Hiraṇyagarbha. That is the meaning of Gāyatrī *mantra* in a nutshell.

In *Rudrādhyāya* (1-7), Lord Śiva is presented as Nīlakaṇṭha (the one with a blue neck):

> असौ योऽवसर्पति नीलग्रीवो विलोहितः ।
>
> *asau yo'vasarpati nīlagrīvo vilohitaḥ* ।
>
> Lord Ṣiva is blue in the neck, but red in the rest of the body. That Lord is rising before us as the Sun.

There is a popular story in the Purāṇas. When the ocean of milk was churned by the gods and the demons, what initially arose was the most virulent poison. On their request, Lord Śiva devoured it and held it in his throat without gulping it, imparting blue colour to the neck. But, we may not cite a Purāṇic story to explain Vedic usage, since it is the Purāṇa that follows the Veda, and not the other way round. The word Nīlagrīva can be understood differently from the point of view of the Cosmic Person. The words *nīla* and *lohita* respectively refer to the blue and red colours of the sky. In fact, Lord Śiva is the Cosmic Person Hiraṇyagarbha, and the Sun is the *adhibhūta* (the gross or the physical) or *adhidaiva* (pertaining to the presiding deity) symbol of the Lord. This *mantra* is describing the rising Sun (*asau yo'vasarpati*). At the time of sunrise and also sunset, the horizon is all red with patches of blue. That horizon is visualised as the neck of the Cosmic Person.

It is normally understood that *Īśvara* is known only to a select few called *ṛṣis*. Common people are not supposed to have the *sākṣātkāra* (direct visualisation) of *Īśvara*. But then the Veda has the opposite to say:

> उतैनं गोपा अदृशन्नदृशन्नुदहार्यः ।
> उतैनं विश्वा भूतानि स दृष्टो मृडयाति नः ।।
>
> — *रुद्राध्यायः, तैत्तिरीय संहिता,* ४-५-१
>
> *utainaṁ gopā adṛśannadṛśannudahāryaḥ* ।
> *utainaṁ viśvā bhūtāni sa dṛṣṭo mṛḍayāti naḥ* ॥
>
> — *Rudrādhyāya, Taittirīya Saṁhitā,* 4-5-1

> Even the cowherds and the women folk carrying water pitchers see this Lord in the form of the Sun. Indeed, all living beings see Him. He is also seen by us. May He protect us.

The cowherds and the women carrying water pitchers on their heads represent the illiterate masses of the countryside. Even they see *Īśvara*. Not only that; every bird, creature, and animal knows the arrival of the *viśvabandhu*, the protector of the entire universe. When the Sun is rising in the east, it is an event recognised by almost every life form, excepting of course, a few people who choose to sleep at that time also!

If there is ever a society in the human history that is very deeply and widely influenced in all aspects of its life by an epic, it is the Hindu society, and that epic is *Śrīmadrāmāyaṇam*. Mother India has no existence without Rāma. Rāma and *Rāmāyaṇa* are the weft and warp of Indian nationhood and the heart and soul of Hindu *dharma*. Vālmīki, the very first poet (*ādikavi*) to compose verses other than the Vedic hymns, is the composer of the immortal epic. That is the reason why this epic is better known as *ādikāvya*, the first poem. Rāma is the hero of the epic. Innumerable poets over centuries have translated or rewritten this great epic in different languages of India. There are quite a few vernacular versions of *Śrīmadrāmāyaṇam* in every language of India. For example, we have the most famous *Tulasī Rāmāyaṇa* in Hindi, *Bhāskara Rāmāyaṇam* and *Molla Rāmāyaṇam* in Telugu, *Kamba Rāmāyaṇam* in Tamil, etc. Even in Sanskrit, we have a few versions of the *Śrīmadrāmāyaṇam* like *Adhyātmarāmāyaṇam* and *Ānandarāmāyaṇam*. There is a fundamental difference between Vālmīki's *Śrīmadrāmāyaṇam* and other versions written by various authors. In all these versions, Rāma is presented even from the very first verse as God, an incarnation of *Īśvara*; but not so in Vālmīki's *Śrīmadrāmāyaṇam* till the very end. Vālmīki portrayed his hero as an ideal human being. If we transform Rāma into God from the very beginning, the value of Rāma as a role model is lost, because we conveniently assume that whatever he has done, only God could have done.

Once, there was a proposal to construct Śivājī Mandir, a temple for the sixteenth-century Hindu Emperor, Śivājī. Some of the *mahātmās* objected to it. Śivājī stands for sacrifice and valour in the face of evil. Their concern is to let Śivājī remain as a role model for the society at least for some more time. If you construct a temple for Śivājī, then Śivājī stops inspiring people. We just do *pūjā* of 108 or even 1008 names, and there it ends. The message of Vālmīki in *Śrīmadrāmāyaṇam* is to live like Rāma, but not like Rāvaṇa. Rāma is presented as a human being, facing all the problems associated with human life, and yet standing upright for the sake of *dharma* in the face of the direst calamity. Rāma was ready to sacrifice everything for upholding *dharma*.

रामो विग्रहवान् धर्मस्साधुस्सत्यपराक्रमः ।

— *श्रीमद्रामायणम्*, ३-३७-१३

rāmo vigrahavān dharmassādhussatyaparākramaḥ ।

— *Śrīmadrāmāyaṇam*, 3-37-13

Rāma is the embodiment of virtuousness. He is a thorough gentleman and a warrior of true valour.

If *dharma* were to take a physical form with a face, hands, legs, etc., it will look like Rāma. This statement was made, not by an admirer of Rāma, but by Mārīca, a demon, who was inimical to Rāma for a long time. Mārīca was the most cunning of the demons. Mārīca is quoted as an example of the most crooked person. It is the greatness of Rāma that he was admired even by his enemies.

Śrīmadrāmāyaṇam is divided into six volumes (*kāṇḍas*) called Bāla, Ayodhyā, Araṇya, Kiṣkindhā, Sundara and Yuddha Kāṇḍas. This *Āditya Hṛdayam* is a small canto (chapter) in Yuddha Kāṇḍa. The context was the battle between Rāma and Rāvaṇa, which was described in glorious detail by the poet Vālmīki. It was a very fierce battle, the fiercest of all the battles of all times. We have no parallel to that battle:

> गगनं गगनाकारं सागरस्सागरोपमः ।
> रामरावणयोर्युद्धं रामरावणयोरिव ।।
>
> *gaganaṁ gaganākāraṁ sāgarassāgaropamaḥ* ।
> *rāmarāvaṇayoryuddhaṁ rāmarāvaṇayoriva* ॥
>
> Sky resembles sky; ocean is like the ocean itself. The battle between Rāma and Rāvaṇa can be compared only with the battle between Rāma and Rāvaṇa.

It was the mother of all battles. In that battle, Rāma was facing the worst of the enemies in Rāvaṇa, who was the most powerful warrior on the face of the earth at that time. Rāvaṇa had all the power and implements of war with him. He was fighting the war in his home turf. He had *sthānabala,* the special advantage that a person gets when he is in his own territory. Rāma came from a faraway place, and was fighting a war in a distant land. Additionally, Rāma was in distress because his dear wife Sītā was kidnapped by Rāvaṇa. It was the world's first episode of kidnapping, of course, not for a ransom. Rāvaṇa initially sent all his war-chiefs, including his ministers, sons, brothers and other followers to fight against Rāma. Rāma destroyed all of them. They were like so many moths attracted and burnt into ashes by the fire called Rāma. Even his invincible brother, Kumbhakarṇa was slain by Rāma in the battlefield. Rāvaṇa came into the battlefield at the fag end of that historic battle. He faced Rāma once in the very beginning of the war, but quickly retreated after tasting the sting of Rāma's arrows. Again, he came at the end since no warrior of repute was left in his camp. Even so, he remained invincible.

Rāma was the greatest of the warriors (*rāmaśśastrabhṛtāṁ varaḥ*). He exterminated a very large number of demons opposing *dharma*. Even so, Rāma was again face to face with a serious problem. His life was full of problems. If everything is comfortable and cozy, following *dharma* is easy. The issue is: when one faces the real test, when adversity stares one in the face, does he follow *dharma* or not? In such a situation, people generally complain: 'O, I have worshipped

Īśvara with devotion; but look what happened to me?' So, Rāma is facing the ultimate crisis of his life and a grand test of his valour and his commitment to *dharma*.

Let us now begin the study of the text, *Āditya Hṛdayam*.

The Original Text

श्रीगणेशाय नमः

श्रीमद्वाल्मीकिरामायणान्तर्गतं

।। आदित्य हृदयम् ।।

[1]

ततो युद्धपरिश्रान्तं समरे चिन्तया स्थितम् ।
रावणं चाग्रतो दृष्ट्वा युद्धाय समुपस्थितम्।।

tato yuddhapariśrāntaṁ samare cintayā sthitam ।
rāvaṇañcāgrato dṛṣṭvā yuddhāya samupasthitam ।।

[2]

दैवतैश्च समागम्य द्रष्टुमभ्यागतो रणम् ।
उपगम्याब्रवीद्राममगस्त्यो भगवानृषिः ।।

daivataiśca samāgamya draṣṭumabhyāgato raṇam ।
upagamyābravīdrāmamagastyo bhagavānṛṣiḥ ।।

[3]

राम राम महाबाहो शृणु गुह्यं सनातनम् ।
येन सर्वानरीन् वत्स समरे विजयिष्यसे ।।

rāma rāma mahābāho śṛṇu guhyaṁ sanātanam ।
yena sarvānarīn vatsa samare vijayiṣyase ।।

[4]

आदित्यहृदयं पु[illegible]ं सर्वशत्रुविनाशनम् ।
जयावहं जपं नित्यमक्ष[illegible]ं परमं शिवम् ।।

ādityahṛdayaṁ puṇyaṁ sarvaśatruvināśanam ।
jayāvahaṁ japaṁ nityamakṣayaṁ paramaṁ śivam ॥

[5]

सर्वमङ्गलमाङ्गल्यं सर्वपापप्रणाशनम् ।
चिन्ताशोकप्रशमनमायुर्वर्धनमुत्तमम् ।।

sarvamaṅgalamāṅgalyaṁ sarvapāpapraṇāśanam ।
cintāśokapraśamanamāyurvardhanamuttamam ॥

[6]

रश्मिमन्तं समुद्यन्तं देवासुरनमस्कृतम् ।
पूजयस्व विवस्वन्तं भास्करं भुवनेश्वरम् ।।

raśmimantaṁ samudyantaṁ devāsuranamaskṛtam ।
pūjayasva vivasvantaṁ bhāskaraṁ bhuvaneśvaram ॥

[7]

सर्वदेवात्मको ह्येष तेजस्वी रश्मिभावनः ।
एष देवासुरगणान् लोकान् पाति गभस्तिभिः ।।

sarvadevātmako hyeṣa tejasvī raśmibhāvanaḥ ।
eṣa devāsuragaṇān lokān pāti gabhastibhiḥ ॥

[8]

एष ब्रह्मा च विष्णुश्च शिवस्स्कन्दः प्रजापतिः ।
महेन्द्रो धनदः कालो यमस्सोमो ह्यपां पतिः ।।

eṣa brahmā ca viṣṇuśca śivasskandaḥ prajāpatiḥ ।
mahendro dhanadaḥ kālo yamassomo hyapāṁ patiḥ ॥

[9]

पितरो वसवस्साध्या अश्विनौ मरुतो मनुः ।
वायुर्वह्निः प्रजाः प्राण ऋतुकर्ता प्रभाकरः ।।

pitaro vasavassādhyā aśvinau maruto manuḥ ।
vāyurvahniḥ prajāḥ prāṇa ṛtukartā prabhākaraḥ ॥

[10]

आदित्यस्सविता सूर्यः खगः पूषा गभस्तिमान् ।
सुवर्णसदृशो भानुर्हिरण्यरेता दिवाकरः ।।

ādityassavitā sūryaḥ khagaḥ pūṣā gabhastimān ।
suvarṇasadṛśo bhānurhiraṇyaretā divākaraḥ ॥

[11]

हरिदश्वस्सहस्रार्चिस्सप्तसप्तिर्मरीचिमान् ।
तिमिरोन्मथनश्शम्भुस्त्वष्टा मार्तण्डकोंऽशुमान् ।।

haridaśvassahasrārcissaptasaptirmarīcimān ।
timironmathanaśśambhustvaṣṭā mārtaṇḍako'ṁśumān ॥

[12]

हिरण्यगर्भश्शिशिरस्तपनोऽहस्करो रविः ।
अग्निगर्भोऽदितेः पुत्रश्शङ्खश्शिशिरनाशनः ।।

hiraṇyagarbhaśśiśirastapano'haskaro raviḥ ।
agnigarbho'diteḥ putraśśaṅkhaśśiśiranāśanaḥ ॥

[13]

व्योमनाथस्तमोभेदी ऋग्यजुस्सामपारगः ।
घनवृष्टिरपां मित्रो विन्ध्यवीथीप्लवङ्गमः ।।

vyomanāthastamobhedī ṛgyajussāmapāragaḥ ।
ghanavṛṣṭirapāṁ mitro vindhyavīthīplavaṅgamaḥ ॥

[14]

आतपी मण्डली मृत्युः पिङ्गलस्सर्वतापनः।
कविर्विश्वो महातेजा रक्तस्सर्वभवोद्भवः।।

ātapī maṇḍalī mṛtyuḥ piṅgalassarvatāpanaḥ ।
kavirviśvo mahātejā raktassarvabhavodbhavaḥ ॥

[15]

नक्षत्रग्रहताराणामधिपो विश्वभावनः।
तेजसामपि तेजस्वी द्वादशात्मन्नमोऽस्तु ते।।

nakṣatragrahatārāṇāmadhipo viśvabhāvanaḥ ।
tejasāmapi tejasvī dvādaśātmannamo'stu te ॥

[16]

नमः पूर्वाय गिरये पश्चिमायाद्रये नमः।
ज्योतिर्गणानां पतये दिनाधिपतये नमः ।।

namaḥ pūrvāya giraye paścimāyādraye namaḥ ।
jyotirgaṇānāṁ pataye dinādhipataye namaḥ ॥

[17]

जयाय जयभद्राय हर्यश्वाय नमो नमः।
नमो नमस्सहस्रांशो आदित्याय नमो नमः।।

jayāya jayabhadrāya haryaśvāya namo namaḥ ।
namo namassahasrāṁśo ādityāya namo namaḥ ॥

[18]

नम उग्राय वीराय सारङ्गाय नमो नमः।
नमः पद्मप्रबोधाय प्रचण्डाय नमोऽस्तु ते।।

nama ugrāya vīrāya sāraṅgāya namo namaḥ ।
namaḥ padmaprabodhāya pracaṇḍāya namo'stu te ॥

[19]

ब्रह्मेशानाच्युतेशाय सूरायादित्यवर्चसे।
भास्वते सर्वभक्षाय रौद्राय वपुषे नमः।।

brahmeśānācyuteśāya sūrāyādityavarcase ।
bhāsvate sarvabhakṣāya raudrāya vapuṣe namaḥ ॥

[20]

तमोघ्नाय हिमघ्नाय शत्रुघ्नायामितात्मने।
कृतघ्नघ्नाय देवाय ज्योतिषां पतये नमः।।

tamoghnāya himaghnāya śatrughnāyāmitātmane ।
kṛtaghnaghnāya devāya jyotiṣāṁ pataye namaḥ ॥

[21]

तप्तचामीकराभाय हरये विश्वकर्मणे।
नमस्तमोऽभिनिघ्नाय रुचये लोकसाक्षिणे।।

taptacāmīkarābhāya haraye viśvakarmaṇe ।
namastamo'bhinighnāya rucaye lokasākṣiṇe ॥

[22]

नाशयत्येष वै भूतं तमेव सृजति प्रभुः।
पायत्येष तपत्येष वर्षत्येष गभस्तिभिः।

nāśayatyeṣa vai bhūtaṁ tameva sr̥jati prabhuḥ ।
pāyatyeṣa tapatyeṣa varṣatyeṣa gabhastibhiḥ ॥

[23]

एष सुप्तेषु जागर्ति भूतेषु परिनिष्ठितः।
एष चैवाग्निहोत्रं च फलं चैवाग्निहोत्रिणाम्।।

eṣa supteṣu jāgarti bhūteṣu pariniṣṭhitaḥ ।
eṣa caivāgnihotraṁ ca phalaṁ caivāgnihotriṇām ॥

[24]

देवाश्च क्रतवश्चैव क्रतूनां फलमेव च।
यानि कृत्यानि लोकेषु सर्वेषु परमप्रभुः।।

devāśca kratavaścaiva kratūnāṁ phalameva ca ।
yāni kr̥tyāni lokeṣu sarveṣu paramaprabhuḥ ॥

[25]

एनमापत्सु कृच्छ्रेषु कान्तारेषु भयेषु च।
कीर्तयन् पुरुषः कश्चिन्नावसीदति राघव।।

enamāpatsu kr̥cchreṣu kāntāreṣu bhayeṣu ca ।
kīrtayan puruṣaḥ kaścinnāvasīdati rāghava ॥

[26]

पूजयस्वैनमेकाग्रो देवदेवं जगत्पतिम्।
एतत् त्रिगुणितं जप्त्वा युद्धेषु विजयिष्यति ।।

pūjayasvainamekāgro devadevaṁ jagatpatim ।
etat triguṇitaṁ japtvā yuddheṣu vijayiṣyati ॥

[27]

अस्मिन् क्षणे महाबाहो रावणं त्वं जहिष्यसि।
एवमुक्त्वा ततोऽगस्त्यो जगाम स यथागतम् ।।

asmin kṣaṇe mahābāho rāvaṇaṁ tvaṁ jahiṣyasi ।
evamuktvā tato'gastyo jagāma sa yathāgatam ॥

[28]

एतच्छ्रुत्वा महातेजा नष्टशोकोऽभवत्तदा।
धारयामास सुप्रीतो राघवः प्रयतात्मवान्।।

etacchrutvā mahātejā naṣṭaśoko'bhavattadā ।
dhārayāmāsa suprīto rāghavaḥ prayatātmavān ॥

[29]

आदित्यं प्रेक्ष्य जप्त्वेदं परं हर्षमवाप्तवान्।
त्रिराचम्य शुचिर्भूत्वा धनुरादाय वीर्यवान्।।

ādityaṁ prekṣya japtvedaṁ paraṁ harṣamavāptavān ।
trirācamya śucirbhūtvā dhanurādāya vīryavān ॥

[30]

रावणं प्रेक्ष्य हृष्टात्मा जयार्थं समुपागमत्।
सर्वयत्नेन महता वृतस्तस्य वधेऽभवत् ।।

rāvaṇaṁ prekṣya hṛṣṭātmā jayārthaṁ samupāgamat ।
sarvayatnena mahatā vṛtastasya vadhe'bhavat ॥

[31]

अथ रविरवदन्निरीक्ष्य रामं मुदितमनाः परमं प्रहृष्यमाणः।
निशिचरपतिसंक्षयं विदित्वा सुरगणमध्यगतो वचस्त्वरेति।।

atha raviravadannirīkṣya rāmaṁ muditamanāḥ paramaṁ prahṛṣyamāṇaḥ ।
niśicarapatisaṅkṣayaṁ viditvā suragaṇamadhyagato vacastvareti ॥

।। इत्यार्षे श्रीमद्रामायणे वाल्मीकीये
आदिकाव्ये युद्धकाण्डे षड्डुत्तरशततमस्सर्गः ।।

॥ *ityārṣe śrīmadrāmāyaṇe vālmīkīye*
ādikāvye yuddhakāṇḍe ṣaḍuttaraśatatamassargaḥ ॥

। श्रीरामचन्द्रार्पणमस्तु ।
। *śrīrāmacanrdārpaṇamastu* ।

The Commentary, Tattvaprakāśikā

[1] & [2]

ततो युद्धपरिश्रान्तं समरे चिन्तया स्थितम् ।
रावणं चाग्रतो दृष्ट्वा युद्धाय समुपस्थितम् ।।

दैवतैश्च समागम्य द्रष्टुमभ्यागतो रणम् ।
उपगम्याब्रवीद्राममगस्त्यो भगवानृषिः ।।

tato yuddhapariśrāntaṁ samare cintayā sthitam |
rāvaṇaṁcāgrato dṛṣṭvā yuddhāya samupasthitam ||

daivataiśca samāgamya draṣṭumabhyāgato raṇam |
upagamyābravīdrāmamagastyo bhagavānṛṣiḥ ||

ततः (*tataḥ*) — afterwards, युद्धपरिश्रान्तम् (*yuddhapariśrāntam*) — exhausted in the battle, समरे (*samare*) — in the battle, चिन्तया (*chintayā*) — with worry, स्थितम् (*sthitam*) — standing, रामम् (*rāmam*) — Rāma, च (*ca*) — and, अग्रतः (*agrataḥ*) — ahead, युद्धाय (*yuddhāya*) — for the battle, समुपस्थितम् (*samupasthitam*) — standing ready, रावणम् (*rāvaṇam*) — Rāvaṇa, दृष्ट्वा (*dṛṣṭvā*) — having seen, दैवतैः समागम्य (*daivataiḥ samāgamya*) — having come together with the gods, रणम् (*raṇam*) — battle, द्रष्टुम् (*dṛṣṭum*) — to see, अभ्यागतः (*abhyāgataḥ*) — having arrived, भगवान् (*bhagavān*) — the revered, अगस्त्यः (*agastyaḥ*) — Agastya, तदा (*tadā*) — then, उपगम्य (*upgamya*) — having approached, अब्रवीत् (*abravīt*) — spoke.

At that time, Rāma was very much exhausted in the battle. While standing in the battlefield, he was filled with worry. The sage Agastya saw him. Agastya arrived there together with the gods to witness the battle. Agastya also saw Rāvaṇa who arrived ready for the battle. The revered sage then approached Rāma and talked to him.

Rāvaṇa, the embodiment of all power, is standing there fully equipped with all the paraphernalia of warfare. Though he was beaten by Rāma on an earlier occasion, he has regained some composure and enthusiasm since then. Rāvaṇa was indeed a great person except for the *adharma* he had committed. He kidnapped Sītā and kept her captive under his control. He did not repent and atone for his misdeed when an opportunity was provided to him. Except for this major sin in his life, he was otherwise a great scholar and devotee of *Īśvara*. What is not there in Rāvaṇa? His wealth, courage, and military strength have no parallel. When Hanumān saw Rāvaṇa for the first time, he was stunned by the brilliance of his countenance and the grandeur of his court. Initially Rāvaṇa ordered that Hanumān be put to death, but when Vibhīṣaṇa told that killing a messenger is an act unworthy of a warrior, he thanked Vibhīṣaṇa for reminding him about *dharma* and rescinded the order. He is quite a formidable enemy.

Rāma is tired and worried. It is like a match point situation in the grand-slam tennis final. If only he wins one more point, he becomes the champion. But by that time, he is extremely tired and he does not have energy even to serve the ball. But then he has to score one more point, and the opponent is ready to grab that point away from him. How desperate he must feel! Rāma's feelings are quite similar at this stage. This Rāvaṇa, the culprit, is there standing before him ready for the battle. He is a great warrior. How to defeat him? It is yet another major crisis in the life of Rāma.

At that time, the gods also came to see this war. And various sages from afar came to see this war. They have the *yoga-śakti* by which they can float in the sky. There are eight *siddhi*s (mystic powers) that seekers may achieve by intense practice of *yoga*. One of the first *siddhi*s is called *aṇimā*; it is the ability to become light and float in air. Sage Agastya noticed Rāma in distress. Here, Agastya is described as *Bhagavān*. It means a very revered sage. It also means that Agastya is an enlightened person. It is well established in the Upaniṣads that the knower of *Brahman* is one with *Brahman*.

> स यो ह वै तत्परमं ब्रह्म वेद ब्रह्मविद् ब्रह्मैव भवति ।
> — *मुण्डकोपनिषत्*, ३-२-९
>
> *sa yo ha vai tatparamaṁ brahma veda brahmavid brahmaiva bhavati* — *Muṇḍakopaniṣat*, 3-2-9
>
> The knower of that Supreme *Brahman* becomes (is) one with *Brahman*.

Lord Kṛṣṇa proclaims in the *Gītā* (7-18):

> ज्ञानी त्वात्मैव मे मतम् ।
> *jñānī tvātmaiva me matam* ।
> It is my final word that the knower of *ātman* is indeed one with me.

Agastya is a great *jñānī*; hence he is called *Bhagavān*. Ramaṇa Maharṣi is also called *Bhagavān* because he is a *jñānī*.

[3]

राम राम महाबाहो शृणु गुह्यं सनातनम् ।
येन सर्वानरीन् वत्स समरे विजयिष्यसे ।।

***rāma rāma mahābāho śṛṇu guhyaṁ sanātanam* ।**
***yena sarvānarīn vatsa samare vijayiṣyase* ॥**

राम राम (*rāma rāma*) — O Rāma, Rāma!, महाबाहो (*mahābāho*) — O mighty armed one!, सनातनम् (*sanātanam*) — eternal, गुह्यम् (*guhyam*) — secret *mantra*, शृणु (*śṛṇu*) — listen (receive), वत्स (*vatsa*) — dear son!, येन (*yena*) — by which, समरे (*samare*) — in the battle, सर्वान् (*sarvān*) — all, अरीन् (*arīn*) — enemies, विजयिष्यसे (*vijayiṣyase*) — will definitely conquer.

> O Rāma, Rāma, you are a mighty armed warrior. Listen my dear. I will initiate you into an eternal secret *mantra* (an encomium of the Lord) by which you will conquer all the enemies in the battle.

There is a lull in the battle, but it is only a calm before the storm. The battle is poised to resume after the rest period. Sage Agastya is waiting for such an opportunity; when he gets that opportunity, he seizes it and comes to Rāma. He addresses him, 'O Rāma, Rāma!' This style of addressing clearly indicates that the blessed sage is anxious to talk to Rāma. He wants to give something to Rāma before the battle with the indefatigable Rāvaṇa resumes. He also addresses him as 'O mighty armed one!' (Mahābāho). Lord Kṛṣṇa addresses Arjuna similarly in the *Gītā* many a time. It originally came from Vālmīki. There is remarkable influence of Vālmīki in Vyāsa's works, especially in the *Mahābhārata*. In poetic style, in the narration of the story, in describing *dharma* and in discussing Upaniṣadic secrets, Vyāsa has emulated Vālmīki. Vālmīki's contribution to the development of the Sanskrit language and literature is immense and unique. Mahā-bāhu is one with mighty arms. Sometimes, the sheer physical strength of the hands and legs may not be enough to win in a given situation. 'O Rāma, be attentive and listen to me. I want to teach you a *mantra*.'

Guhya or *rahasya* (secret) implies a *mantra*, because *mantra* is considered very valuable to the seeker in his journey to the Reality. The seeker is supposed to hold on to it in his heart for the lifetime. One should not go around telling that he has done the *japa* (recitation) of this or that *mantra*. This *mantra* is *sanātana*, eternal, which means that it has its origin in the Vedas. *Śrīmadrāmāyaṇam* very closely resembles the Vedic literature in its content, dictum, and idiom. In fact, it is said:

> वेदवेद्ये परे पुंसि जाते दशरथात्मजे ।
> वेदः प्राचेतसादासीत् साक्षाद्रामायणात्मना ।।

> *vedavedye pare puṁsi jāte daśarathātmaje* ।
> *vedaḥ prācetasādāsīt sākṣādrāmāyaṇātmanā* ॥

> When the Cosmic Person known through the teachings of the Vedas is born as Rāma, the son of Daśaratha, the Veda itself took the incarnation of *Śrīmadrāmāyaṇam* through Vālmīki.

This is the reason why the worship of Hiraṇyagarbha in the solar orb, which is the hallmark of Vedic culture, is presented in its totality in the *Śrīmadrāmāyaṇam*. In *Śrīmadrāmāyaṇam*, as in the Vedas, Viṣṇu is the Sun. Viṣṇu means the all-pervading *Īśvara*. He is in the form of the Sun before us. That is why the Sun is also called Sūryanārāyaṇa. In fact, *Bhagavān* says in the *Gītā* (10-21):

> आदित्यानामहं विष्णुः ।
> *ādityānāmahaṁ viṣṇuḥ* ।
>
> I am Viṣṇu among the offspring of Aditi.

We may think that probably the *mantra* could wait for some other occasion! Rāma is now in the midst of a battle. Is this the time for a *mantra*? Agastya addresses Rāma with all love and affection: 'My dear boy, come near me. I will teach this *mantra* to you with the help of which you will be able to vanquish your enemies.'

[4]

आदित्यहृदयं पुण्यं सर्वशत्रुविनाशनम् ।
जयावहं जपं नित्यमक्षयं परमं शिवम् ॥

***ādityahṛdayaṁ puṇyaṁ sarvaśatruvināśanam* ।**
***jayāvahaṁ japaṁ nityamakṣayaṁ paramaṁ śivam* ॥**

आदित्यहृदयम् (*ādityahṛdayaṁ*) — Ādityahṛdayaṁ, जपम् (*japam*) — the *mantra* or *stotra* (encomium), पुण्यम् (*puṇyam*) — sacred, सर्वशत्रुविनाशनम् (*sarvaśatruvināśanam*) — one which helps to vanquish all the enemies, जय-आवहम् (*jaya-āvaham*) — one which secures victory, नित्यम् (*nityam*) — eternal, अक्षयम् (*akṣayam*) — unfailing, परमम् (*paramam*) — supreme, शिवम् (*śivam*) — auspicious.

Listen to this sacred and eternal *mantra* or *stotra* (encomium) called *Āditya-Hṛdayam*. It will help you gain victory by vanquishing all the enemies. It is unfailing and supremely auspicious.

Sage Agastya says: I will teach you a *stotra* which is called *Āditya-Hṛdayam*. The name *Āditya-Hṛdayam* is very significant. This *stotra* is an elaborate description of the Lord in the form of Āditya, the Sun. Also, there is no essential difference between Āditya, the presiding deity of the solar orb that is before our eyes, and the *ātman*, the awareness obtaining in this body; and that *ātman* is visualised in *upāsanā* in the heart, *hṛdayam*. In the Vedic culture, if you ask the question, where the Lord is?, the answer is:

अणोरणीयान् महतो महीयानात्मा गुहायां निहितोऽस्य जन्तोः।

— *महानारायणोपनिषत्*, १०

aṇoraṇīyān mahato mahīyānātmā guhāyāṁ nihito'sya jantoḥ । — *Mahānārāyaṇopaniṣat*, 10

The *ātman*, which is smaller than the smallest and bigger than the biggest, abides in this living being in the cave of the heart.

That is the address of *Īśvara*. He abides in the cave of the intellect in all living beings. So, *Īśvara* has now got two addresses; one is the Sun, and the other is the Heart. Thus, this *stotra* which elucidates the meaning of Gāyatrī *mantra*, is named very appropriately as *Āditya-Hṛdayam*. This is *puṇya*; it sanctifies the seeker who recites it. When the Sun rises in the eastern horizon, the entire globe is sanctified because of it. Dirty places remain dirty, if enough sunlight does not come in. The seeker's mind becomes free of impurities like suffering by reciting this *stotra*.

Sarvaśatruvināśanam. Visualise the glory of *Īśvara* in the solar orb, and also contemplate upon that *Īśvara* in your heart. It gives you a wonderful freshness and purity of heart with the help of which you can overcome all the internal enemies. What are these enemies? *Kāma* (desire), *krodha* (anger), *lobha* (greed), *moha* (infatuation), *mada* (arrogance), and *mātsarya* (jealousy). This group of the six internal enemies is called *ariṣaḍvarga*. In life too, it is a Rāma-Rāvaṇa battle everyday, because life is full of conflicts and problems. Nobody has an easy life. By the recitation of this *stotra*, the spirit of *dharma* is instilled in the heart of the seeker, so that he can face the battles of life with courage and determination without violating *dharma*. That is the significance of teaching the *Gītā Āditya-Hṛdayam* in the battlefield. It is not a teaching that is done in a cave in Uttara Kāśī or some isolated place. It is not a teaching that is exclusively meant for some renunciates. It is for the people who are engaged in the battle of life.

Jayāvaham: Recitation of this *stotra* gives us victory by destroying these enemies, internal and external. External enemies are in the form of various obstacles in the way of progress. Internal enemies are misplaced emotional values and a wrong value structure. A man is a slave to his own internal value structure. He cannot live an independent life, because he imprisons himself in this value structure. So he needs support to overcome these impediments; the recitation of this *stotra* provides the required support. If memorised, it takes less than ten minutes to recite these verses. One may do so on a daily basis. One can also easily recite it in a journey. Ideally, you may stand before the rising Sun and recite it.

Akṣayam, immortal and unfailing. *Brahman* is *akṣaya*. Therefore the encomium of *Brahman* is also *akṣaya*.

Śivam, very auspicious. There are some things that are very auspicious. *Tilaka* on the forehead is auspicious. Prostrating before the Lord is an auspicious act. Paying respect to the elders and receiving their blessing is also auspicious. Charity is auspicious. Life should have an auspicious value structure. A good photograph in the house is auspicious. The moment you enter a house and see a picture of Lord Kṛṣṇa teaching the *Gītā*. That is auspicious. Auspiciousness has to be maintained in life. Reciting these verses is very auspicious, because it brings prosperity here and hereafter.

[5]

सर्वमङ्गलमाङ्गल्यं सर्वपापप्रणाशनम् ।
चिन्ताशोकप्रशमनमायुर्वर्धनमुत्तमम् ।।

sarvamaṅgalamāṅgalyaṁ sarvapāpapraṇāśanam ।
cintāśokapraśamanamāyurvardhanamuttamam ॥

सर्वमङ्गलमाङ्गल्यम् (*sarvamaṅgalamāṅgalyam*) — the most auspicious among the auspicious things, सर्वपापप्रणाशनम् (*sarvapāpapraṇāśanam*) — one which completely destroys all the evil propensities, चिन्ताशोकप्रशमनम् (*cintāśokapraśamanam*) — one which mitigates the worry and affliction, आयुर्वर्धनम् (*āyurvardhanam*) — one which enhances the lifespan, उत्तमम् (*uttamam*) — the best.

This *stotra* is the most auspicious among the auspicious. It completely destroys all the evil propensities in the seeker and thus mitigates the worry and affliction. It enhances the lifespan of the seeker. It is the best encomium.

There are many auspicious things in the world. Which is the best among all? We have a verse that sets this doubt to rest.

अतिकल्याणरूपत्वात् नित्यकल्याणसंश्रयात् ।
स्मर्तॄणां वरदत्वाच्च ब्रह्म तन्मङ्गलं परम् ।।

atikalyāṇarūpatvāt nityakalyāṇasaṁśrayāt ।
smartṝṇāṁ varadatvācca brahma tanmaṅgalaṁ param ॥

That *Brahman* is the embodiment of supreme auspiciousness. It is the eternal source of all auspiciousness. People who dwell upon it are blessed by it. Hence, That *Brahman* is the auspiciousness supreme.

Any reference to *Brahman* is auspicious. In the beginning of the *Brahmasūtra Bhāṣya*, Śrī Śaṅkara did not compose the customary verse of prayer. Hence, an objection is raised: this work cannot be auspicious, since the prayer is missing. This argument is refuted thus: here, Śrī Śaṅkara refers to *ātman*, which is non-different from *Brahman*. There cannot be anything more auspicious than that. Every other thing becomes auspicious by association with *Brahman*. That *Brahman* is before us in the solar orb. Standing before the Sun itself is the most auspicious thing. What to speak of reciting these verses?

Sarvapāpapraṇāśanam. When the devotee contemplates upon the Sun in his heart while reciting these verses, all wrong thoughts disappear and the mind immediately gets purified. In fact, it can take the seeker to the level of knowledge of *Brahman* Itself.

Cintāśokapraśamanam. Every human being is generally afflicted with two things. One is worry and fear about the future (*cintā*), and therefore we suffer from a sense of insecurity. The other is sorrow about the past (*śoka*). We carry the past into the present in the form of sorrow. All good things of the past are readily forgotten; only the bad things are remembered. We have a problem associated with the present also. It is *moha*, the delusion, the absence of discrimination (*viveka*). We take non-*ātman* as *ātman* and vice versa. This is not a condemnation of human existence. It is just a statement of fact. Human nature is like that. Every human being suffers from them. So condemnation solves nothing. You recognise the fact and seek a solution. Here is the solution. You recite *Āditya-Hṛdayam* regularly and contemplate upon *Īśvara*; your afflictions and worries are then gone by the grace of *Īśvara*.

Āyurvardhanam. Scriptures say that we may desire to gain health by propitiating to the Lord Sun.

> आरोग्यं भास्करादिच्छेत् ।
> *ārogyaṁ bhāskarādicchet* ।
>
> One may aspire for good health from the Sun.

Health is wealth. What would one prefer? Health with a modest bank balance or illness with a fat bank balance? Of course, the former. If one has to visit a hospital, one hundred thousand rupees amount to nothing. Just paying for the diagnostic tests will exhaust that amount. So, good health is equal to a lot of wealth. There can be no better wealth than the health. If we worship the Sun everyday in the morning by offering *arghya* (water sanctified by the recitation of Gāyatrī *mantra*), followed by the chanting of these verses, as already mentioned, the mind becomes purified. When the mind is pure and cheerful, the body becomes healthy automatically. If the seeker persists in his unflinching devotion, mundane benefits like prosperity, good health, etc., will automatically accrue to him. Health comes natural to the person who worships *Īśvara* in the form of the Sun both in the morning and evening. Basically, health is in the mind. Suppose one gets up in the morning feeling dull and does not feel like taking bath. So he drinks a cup of coffee and reads newspaper or watches TV. That is the sign of ill-health. On the other hand, suppose one gets up from the bed enthusiastically, takes bath, propitiates the Lord Sun by reciting these verses; that is good health. There is no other health. Of course, there may be some problems of the physical body to be taken care of. But the doctor will also be able to help more effectively if one has this attitude. If the person does not have a proper value system, the doctor's efforts also get defeated many times. Regular exercise is good for health; taking proper medicine at the time of need is good for health; *Āditya-Hṛdayam* does not replace them. It is *uttama*, the best support in life. One should have prayer as an integral part of life.

[6]

रश्मिमन्तं समुद्यन्तं देवासुरनमस्कृतम् ।
पूजयस्व विवस्वन्तं भास्करं भुवनेश्वरम् ।।

raśmimantaṁ samudyantaṁ devāsura-namaskṛtam |
pūjayasva vivasvantaṁ bhāskaraṁ bhuva-neśvaram ||

रश्मिमन्तम् (*raśmimantam*) — the one with rays, समुद्यन्तम् (*samudyantam*) — rising swiftly, देवासुरनमस्कृतम् (*devāsuranamaskṛtam*) — the one who is propitiated by gods and demons, विवस्वन्तम् (*vivasvantam*) — the one who dispels darkness or the one who is the repository of wealth, भुवनेश्वरम् (*bhuvaneśvaram*) — the overlord of all worlds, भास्करम् (*bhāskaram*) — the Sun, पूजयस्व (*pūjayasva*) — worship him.

You worship the Sun. As He rises swiftly with his rays, even gods and demons propitiate Him. He dispels the darkness. He is the ultimate source of all wealth. He is the Overlord of all the worlds.

Sage Agastya advises Rāma, who is the greatest of warriors and an incarnation of Viṣṇu thus: *pūjayasva vivasvantam*, worship the Sun! What to speak of common people like us! One can imagine how much more applicable this advice is to common people like us.

Vivasvantam, vivāsanavantam, one who drives away the darkness. Like light darkness is twofold; the outer and the inner (ignorance). By worshipping the Sun, the seeker, in addition to gaining good physical health, can also overcome the dullness of mind. Vivasvān also means, *viśeṣeṇa vasumān*, the one who has immense wealth. The Sun is the ultimate source of all wealth.

Here a few names of the Sun are given. The names of God are indeed the attributes of God. It is not so for us. A person, who did not offer one drop of *soma* in the fire, may be named *somayājī* (one who performed the ritual called *somayāga*), if his grandfather happens to be one. *Nāmasaṅkīrtana*, recitation of the names of the Lord with devotion, is one of the most important ways of worshipping the Lord. But one may preferably know the meaning of the names.

Raśmimantaṁ samudyantam. The Sun, as He rises in the east, is the repository of rays and energy. There is a *mantra* with similar description recited in *sandhyā-vandanā*:

उदुत्यं जातवेदसं देवं वहन्ति केतवः । दृशे विश्वाय सूर्यम् ।।

— *तैत्तिरीय संहिता*, ४-४३

udutyaṁ jātavedasaṁ devaṁ vahanti ketavaḥ ।
dṛśe viśvāya sūryam ।।

— *Taittirīya Saṁhitā*, 4-43

> The rays are bringing out the Sun, who is the fire in the outer space (who is the origin of Vedic knowledge) from down below to the higher sky, thereby enabling all living beings to have a glimpse of Him.

Devāsuranamaskṛtam. *Deva*s are the gods or angels and *asura*s are the demons. The well-known *deva*s like Indra, Varuṇa, Yama, etc., worship the Sun, who is the symbol of the Cosmic Person. *Asura*s like Virocana also worship the Lord in the solar orb. This is *adhidaiva* meaning. Also, both *deva*s and *asura*s live in our midst. *Deva*s are the people of wisdom, people who serve the society. *Asura*s are the bad people, like smugglers, rowdies, etc., who harm the society. These *deva*s, namely the sages, the wise and the pious, are all worshipping the Sun as He rises in the east. Even *asura*s worship the Sun in a way. They too seek the grace of the Lord for the success of their evil designs. They are also waiting for the Sun to rise to begin their nefarious activities. This is *adhibhūta* meaning. These *deva*s and *asura*s are actually within us. *Deva*s are the good thoughts and *asura*s are the opposite. Both kinds of thoughts have their existence in the *ātman*, the Awareness. *Deva*s are the sense-organs. When they indulge in carnal pleasures, they are called *asura*s (*asuṣu ramante iti*). In any case, they derive their energy from the Sun alone. They function in the Awareness that is *ātman* alone. This is the *adhyātma* meaning.

Bhāskaram, one who gives illumination. The Sun soaks the entire world with his light. The illumination is twofold: the outer, in which we are able to see all objects; the inner, the light of awareness in which all knowledge takes place. The Sun abides in the cave of the heart of the seeker as the awareness that is *ātman* and illuminates various mind modifications. He blesses the sense-organs and the organs of actions with their respective functions.

Bhuvaneśvaram, the overlord of all the worlds. This entire universe is nourished and protected by the Cosmic Person, who abides in the solar orb. All the life forms on earth are under the overall protection and control of the Sun.

[7]

सर्वदेवात्मको ह्येष तेजस्वी रश्मिभावनः ।
एष देवासुरगणान् लोकान् पाति गभस्तिभिः ।।

***sarvadevātmako hyeṣa tejasvī raśmibhāvanaḥ* ।**
***eṣa devāsuragaṇān lokān pāti gabhastibhiḥ* ॥**

तेजस्वी (*tejasvī*) — brilliant, रश्मिभावनः (*raśmibhāvanaḥ*) — the one who creates and protects with his rays, एषः (*eśaḥ*) — this Sun, सर्वदेवात्मकः हि (*sarvadevātmakaḥ hi*) — is indeed the embodiment of all gods, एषः (*eśaḥ*) — this Sun, देवासुरगणान् (*devāsurgaṇān*) — the groups of gods and demons, लोकान् (*lokān*) — their worlds, गभस्तिभिः (*gabhastibhiḥ*) — with the rays, पाति (*pāti*) — safeguards.

This brilliant Sun alone is in the form of all the gods. He illuminates all the objects of the world with his rays. He protects the groups of gods and demons and their worlds with his rays.

Eṣaḥ, this Sun. The word *eṣaḥ* is used when a thing in front is pointed. This verse points out that *Īśvara* is in front of us in the form of the brilliant Sun. How can anyone say that *Īśvara* is not around? People want to see *Īśvara*. A devotee approached a *Mahātmā* with a desire to see *Īśvara*. The *Mahātmā* wanted to know what kind of *Īśvara* does he desire to see. He wants to see *Īśvara* holding conch, discus, mace and sword in his four hands. The *Mahātmā* asked the devotee: 'OK, I will show that *Īśvara* to you. What will you do with that *Īśvara*? *Īśvara* is there before us as the Sun. You have done nothing about it. You are blind to that *Īśvara*. *Īśvara* is there very much before us. But we fail to recognise Him. What a misfortune!

Sarvadevātmako hyeṣaḥ. The Sun stands for Hiraṇyagarbha, the Cosmic Person. All gods like Indra, Varuṇa, Agni, etc., are so many limbs of that Cosmic Person, since each god is an expression of the Universal Power.

Raśmibhāvanaḥ. The Sun creates and sustains life on this planet with his rays. There is creation all around us. The blades of grass sprout from the earth. Plants bear flowers and fruits. All this process of creation is in place because of the Sun's rays.

The Sun protects and nurtures all the gods and demons. The Sun is a *karmayogī*. He does not discriminate between the good and the evil. A *mantra* of *Vājasaneya-Saṁhitā* (36-18) advises the human beings thus:

> मित्रस्य चक्षुषा सर्वाणि भूतानि समीक्षन्ताम् ।
> *mitrasya cakṣuṣā sarvāṇi bhūtāni samīkṣantām* ।
>
> You may have the vision of the Sun towards all life forms.

The Sun gives light and warmth to good and bad people alike. A carnivorous animal gets its energy from the Sun. Herbivorous animals like cow also get their energy from the Sun. We should learn from this to avoid judging others. We should recognise the universal *ātman* in all people. We should recognise *Īśvara* in all life forms.

[8]

एष ब्रह्मा च विष्णुश्च शिवस्स्कन्दः प्रजापतिः ।
महेन्द्रो धनदः कालो यमस्सोमो ह्यपां पतिः ।।

***eṣa brahmā ca viṣṇuśca śivasskandaḥ prajā-patiḥ* ।**
***mahendro dhanadaḥ kālo yamassomo hyapāṁ patiḥ* ॥**

एषः हि (*eṣaḥ hi*) — This Sun indeed is, ब्रह्मा (*brahmā*) — the creator, विष्णुः (*viṣṇuḥ*) — the sustainer, च (*ca*) — and, शिवः (*śivaḥ*) — the most auspicious, स्कन्दः (*skandaḥ*) — the life force or the Lord Kumāra, प्रजापतिः (*prajāpatiḥ*) — the overlord of all life forms, महेन्द्रः (*mahandraḥ*) — the ultimate source of all strength or Lord Indra, धनदः (*dhanadaḥ*) — one who gives wealth, or Lord Kubera, कालः (*kālaḥ*) — the originator of time, or one who is in the form of time, यमः (*yamaḥ*) — the controller, or Lord Yama, सोमः (*somaḥ*) — the Lord together with the Universal Power, or Lord Moon, अपां पतिः (*apāṁ patiḥ*) — the Lord of waters, or Varuṇa.

This, the most auspicious Sun, indeed is the creator and sustainer of the universe. He is the life force of this universe. He is Lord Kumāra. He is the overlord of all life. He is the ultimate source of all strength as Lord Indra. He is the giver of all wealth as Lord Kubera. As the God of Time, he is the originator of time. He controls all life as Lord Yama. He is the Godhead endowed with the Universal Power. He is Lord Moon. He is the Lord of waters, Varuṇa.

People talk of trinity. Descriptions of Brahmā, Viṣṇu and Rudra are taken literally by people. They think that there are really three persons identified by those names. These three persons also seem to be engaged in mutual confrontation. But the *Taittirīyopaniṣat* (3-1) says:

यतो वा इमानि भूतानि जायन्ते । येन जातानि जीवन्ति।
यत्प्रयन्त्यभिसंविशन्ति । तद्विजिज्ञासस्व । तद्ब्रह्मेति ।।

yato vā imāni bhūtāni jāyante । *yena jātāni jīvanti* ।
yatprayantyabhisaṁviśanti । *tadvijijñāsasva* ।
tadbrahmeti ।।

Desire to know That, from which all the things of the Universe have originated, by which they are sustained, and into which they resolve. That is *Brahman*.

So, the Godhead is defined as the One who/which creates, sustains and annihilates this universe. The Ultimate Reality is one, not three. Vālmīki says that this Sun alone is Brahmā, Viṣṇu and Rudra. All life on earth derives its existence from the rays of the Sun. The Sun who sustains life by giving heat and light is Viṣṇu. The Sun causes time, and thus brings death to all life forms. When the Sun becomes cool, all creation comes to an end.

Skandaḥ. The particular aspect of *Īśvara* in the form of energy is called Skanda. That Skanda, the God of energy, is before us as the Sun.

Prajāpatiḥ, the progenitor of all life forms in this world. In the Vedic scheme of creation, in the first step, the Cosmic Person manifests by His will as Manu, are carries the creation forward. This Manu is called a Prajāpati. Being the offspring of the Cosmic Person, he is one with Him. Accordingly, the Sun is also identified with Prajāpati.

Dhanadaḥ, the one who gives wealth. An oil tycoon in Texas is a billionnaire because of the oil wealth. Where did this oil come from? The Sun god has given all the oil in the world. Agricultural produce is another important source of riches. Once again, the Sun is the source of that wealth. Nowadays, sports and games are a great source of wealth. Players of tennis, soccer, etc., make millions. Their health and vigour of the body is the source of wealth for them. That health and vigour is once again gained from the Lord Sun. In this world, there is only one source of all wealth. And that is *Īśvara* in the form of the Sun.

He is *kāla*, the death. *Taittirīya Āraṇyaka* (1-14) describes thus:

> योऽसौ तपन्नुदेति। स सर्वेषां भूतानां प्राणानादायोदेति। —
> असौ योऽस्तमेति। स सर्वेषां भूतानां प्राणानादायास्तमेति।।
>
> *yo'sau tapannudeti । sa sarveṣāṁ bhūtānāṁ prāṇānādāyodeti । — asau yo'stameti । sa sarveṣāṁ bhūtānāṁ prāṇānādāyāstameti ॥*
>
> This Sun is rising. While doing so, He is taking away the life forces of all living beings. — The Sun is setting. While doing so, He is drawing towards Him the vital energies of all the life forms.

Here is the Sun rising. What a beautiful sight! Poets write poems on the rising Sun. But, every time the Sun rises, he reduces our lifespan somewhat. Similarly, while setting, the Sun withdraws another small part from the lives of all living beings. The process of ageing and ripening is caused by the rays of the Sun. The fruit ripens only to fall down. Body is ripening, and the cells are ageing. That is all the handiwork of the Sun. The Lord of Death is not hiding anywhere. He is there right in front of us as the Sun. In the Purāṇas, the Lord of Death is presented as the son of Lord Sun. In Vedānta, we learn to smile at death, because the Lord of death is himself the teacher of this knowledge. Death can teach us much that life can never teach. People consider death as a cataclysmic event, and they are aghast when it occurs. That is not correct. Lord Kṛṣṇa presents death in its true perspective in the *Gītā* (2-27):

> जातस्य हि ध्रुवो मृत्युर्ध्रुवं जन्म मृतस्य च ।
> *jātasya hi dhruvo mṛtyurdhruvaṁ janma mṛtasya ca* ।
>
> The one who is born is bound to die, and the one who dies is bound to take birth again.

We consider death as inauspicious, because we are afraid of death. But, Lord Rudra, the destroyer of the universe, resides in the cremation ground. There is nothing inauspicious about it. All this universe is a manifestation of *Brahman* alone. In this creation, either everything is inauspicious because everything is unreal (*mithyā*), or everything is auspicious because everything is *Brahman*.

The Sun is called *kāla*, the Time, because there is an important oneness between time and the Sun. The Sun is the origin of the concept of time itself. This aspect is described in the *Taittirīya Āraṇyaka* (1-2) as follows:

> सूर्यो मरीचिमादत्ते । सर्वस्माद्भुवनादधि । तस्याः पाकविशेषेण । स्मृतं कालविशेषणम् ।।
> *sūryo marīcimādatte* । *sarvasmādbhuvanādadhi* ।
> *tasyāḥ pāka-viśeṣeṇa* । *smṛtaṁ kālaviśeṣaṇam* ॥
>
> The Sun spreads his rays over all the world. The rays produce chemical changes, which define the changes in time.

Yamaḥ, yamayati iti, one who controls. The Sun controls everything including time, the seasons, the flow of the rivers, the weather patterns, the oceans, the ocean currents, etc.

Apāṁ patiḥ, the overlord of waters. All flora and fauna depend on water. Water is indeed life. Thus, it is possible to recognise *Īśvara* in every aspect of life. Such a recognition makes life easy, simple, and auspicious.

[9]

पितरो वसवस्साध्या अश्विनौ मरुतो मनुः ।
वायुर्वह्निः प्रजाः प्राण ऋतुकर्ता प्रभाकरः ।।

***pitaro vasavassādhyā aśvinau maruto manuḥ* ।**
***vāyurvahniḥ prajāḥ prāṇa ṛtukartā prabhākaraḥ* ।।**

पितरः (*pitaraḥ*) — the manes, वसवः (*vasavaḥ*) — the Vasus, साध्याः (*sādhyāḥ*) — the Sādhyas, अश्विनौ (*aśvinau*) — the Aśvinis, मरुतः (*marutaḥ*) — the Maruts, मनुः (*manuḥ*) — the progenitor Manu, वायुः (*vāyuḥ*) — the wind god, वह्निः (*vahniḥ*) — the fire god, प्रजाः (*prajāḥ*) — the life forms, प्राणः (*prāṇaḥ*) — the life force, ऋतुकर्ता (*ṛtukartā*) — the maker of seasons, प्रभाकरः (*prabhākaraḥ*) — the source of all illumination.

The manes, Vasus, Sādhyas, Aśvinis, Maruts, Manu, the wind god, the fire god are one with the Sun. The Sun is indeed the Cosmic Power and He alone manifests as all these life forms. The Sun, who illuminates everything, causes the seasons.

Pitaraḥ, our ancestors, who are in majority. The Sun with the name Aryaman represents all the manes. The ancestral rites are generally performed when the Sun is at its full brilliance, namely, at noon.

Vasavaḥ, the Vasus, a group of eight gods. Agni (god of fire) is one of them. All gods represent various limbs of Hiraṇyagarbha, the Sun.

Sādhyas are another group of gods. The Vedas describe many such groups of gods. All these gods are indeed several limbs of the Universal Person represented by the Sun. Sādhya also means a *yogī*, the seeker who practices *yoga*. All such seekers are identified with the Sun.

Aśvinau are the smallest of the groups of gods, consisting of only two gods. They are the divine physicians. If Indra gets a stomach pain, he sends for them.

Marutaḥ. Maruts constitute another group of forty-nine gods. Together they constitute what is called Wind God. Wind blows ever from one corner of the globe to the other, thus keeping the life forms alive. This huge energy of the wind is once again derived from the Sun alone.

Manuḥ, manute iti; one who knows everything. In the *Gītā*, the fourth chapter opens as follows:

> श्रीभगवानुवाच ।
> इमं विवस्वते योगं प्रोक्तवानहमव्ययम् ।
> विवस्वान् मनवे प्राह मनुरिक्ष्वाकवेऽब्रवीत् ।।
>
> *śrībhagavānuvāca* ।
> *imaṁ vivasvate yogaṁ proktavānahamavyayam* ।
> *vivasvān manave prāha manurikṣvākave'bravīt* ॥
>
> The blessed Lord spoke thus: I gave this knowledge at the time of creation to Lord Sun, who in turn gave it to Manu, and who in turn gave it to Ikṣvāku.

This is the reason why the Sun is considered as omniscient. It is said that the sage Yājñavalkya, the seer of *Yajurveda*, gained all that knowledge from the Sun. Also, there is a clan of kings after the Sun god and Lord Rāma belongs to that clan. Sage Agastya was advising Rāma to propitiate the originator of his own clan, the Sun. Manu is talked about as the son of the Sun as well as of the Cosmic Person, because of the essential identity between the two. Manu is the progenitor of all life forms. The human being is named after him as *mānava*, the offspring of Manu. In the *Bṛhadāraṇyakopaniṣat* (1-4-3), it is described that Hiraṇyagarbha, the creator, created at first Manu and Śatarūpā by dividing himself into the two of them.

Vāyuḥ, the wind god, or the life force pervading this body, is also a manifestation of the Sun alone.

Vahniḥ, vahati iti, One who contains the essence of all life within Himself. Vahni is also the fire. The *Taittirīya Āraṇyaka* (1-20) gives a very interesting description of Aditi, the Universal Power as follows:

> आदित्यस्सर्वोऽग्निः पृथिव्याम् । वायुरन्तरिक्षे । सूर्यो दिवि । चन्द्रमा दिक्षु । नक्षत्राणि स्वलोके ।।
>
> *ādityassarvo'gniḥ pṛthivyām* । *vāyurantarikṣe* ।
> *sūryo divi* । *candramā dikṣu* । *nakṣatrāṇi svaloke* ॥
>
> All fire on earth, the wind in the atmosphere, the Sun in the interstellar space, the moon moving around the earth in the quarters, and the stars in their respective galactical positions are indeed the manifestations of Aditi, the Universal Power.

Prajāḥ, prajāyante iti, all forms of life. The entire life on this planet is solely dependent on the heat and light of the Sun. *Encyclopedia of Science and Technology* (vol. 10, p. 184; McGraw-Hill, New York, 1966) gives the following graphic account of how the Sun sustains this globe:

> Photosynthesis is one particularly important natural process. It involves the manufacture, in light, of organic compounds (primarily carbohydrates) from inorganic materials with simultaneous liberation of oxygen, by chlorophyll-containing plant cells. — The light energy taken by the green pigment, chlorophyll, is partially converted by photosynthesis into stored chemical energy. Together, the two aspects of photosynthesis — the conversion of inorganic into organic matter and the conversion of light

energy into chemical energy — make it the fundamental process of life on earth. It is the unique source of all living matter and of all life on our planet. The elements carbon, oxygen, and hydrogen are exchanged through photosynthesis in an endless cycle between the organic and inorganic worlds. Therefore, life on earth can be maintained only by the constant supply of solar energy and its utilisation through plant photosynthesis.

Prāṇaḥ, prāṇayati iti. The entire motive power and the power of thinking in the living beings of this world comes from the Sun. That is why the Sun is the best representative of the Universal Person (Hiraṇyagarbha or *Īśvara*) and the eastern horizon is His best temple. This fact was recognised by the ancient Vedic sages. Agastya advises Rāma to worship the Sun rising in the eastern skies.

Generally, we take the life in the body as an independent entity. This is not true. The body is alive, because the Universal Power reflects in it. That Universal Power called *prāṇa* has its origin in the *para-Brahman*. This point is beautifully explained in a verse in the *Kaṭhopaniṣat* (2-2-1).

न प्राणेन नापानेन मर्त्यो जीवति कश्चन ।
इतरेण तु जीवन्ति यस्मिन्नेतावुपाश्रितौ ।।

na prāṇena nāpānena martyo jīvati kaścana ।
itareṇa tu jīvanti yasminnetāvupāśritau ॥

No mortal person is alive because of inhalation and exhalation. All living beings are alive because of that Universal Power (or the *Brahman* from which it originates). The inhalation and exhalation are in place because of that Power.

Ṛtukartā, the maker of the seasons. Different seasons like autumn, spring, etc., obviously owe their origin to the Sun.

Prabhākaraḥ, a synonym to Bhāskaraḥ.

[10]

आदित्यस्सविता सूर्यः खगः पूषा गभस्तिमान् ।
सुवर्णसदृशो भानुर्हिरण्यरेता दिवाकरः ।।

***ādityassavitā sūryaḥ khagaḥ pūṣā gabhastimān* ।**
***suvarṇasadṛśo bhānurhiraṇyaretā divākaraḥ* ॥**

आदित्यः (*ādityaḥ*) — the offspring of Aditi, सविता (*savitā*) — the creator, सूर्यः (*sūryaḥ*) — the Sun, खगः (*khagaḥ*) — one who travels in the outer space, पूषा (*pūṣā*) — one who nourishes, गभस्तिमान् (*gabhastimān*) — one who has multitude of rays, सुवर्णसदृशः (*suvarṇadṛśaḥ*) — one who resembles pure gold, भानुः (*bhānuḥ*) — the shining, हिरण्यरेताः (*hiraṇyaretāḥ*) — the energy-seed of the universe, दिवाकरः (*divākaraḥ*) — one who causes daybreak.

The Sun, son of Aditi, the creator of all life, pervades all. He is the traveller in the sky, nourisher of all life and the source of all light. He shines golden yellow (early in the morning). He is the energy which was the seed of this universe. He causes the day and night.

Ādityaḥ, the son of Aditi. In the Purāṇas, Aditi is described as the mother of all gods. This Aditi of the Purāṇas is indeed a symbolic representation of the Universal Power. It is thus described in the *Kaṭhopaniṣat* (2-1-7):

या प्राणेन संभवत्यदितिर्देवतामयी ।
गुहां प्रविश्य तिष्ठन्तीं या भूतेभिर्व्यजायत ।।

yā prāṇena saṁbhavatyaditirdevatāmayī ।
guhāṁ praviśya tiṣṭhantīṁ yā bhūtebhirvyajāyata ॥

Aditi (the Universal Power), the embodiment of all gods, has manifested (from *para-Brahman*) as Hiraṇyagarbha together with the great basic

> elements (or all life forms). She is established in the cave of the heart of the living beings.

It is indeed in the fitness of things to describe the Sun as the offspring of that Aditi. According to the Big Bang theory of creation of the modern cosmologists, there was a primordial ylem of infinite energy and density before creation. When that ball exploded, galaxies of stars were created. Aditi corresponds to the energy of that Primordial principle.

Savitā, the creator. *Īśvara* is described as Savitā in Gāyatrī *mantra* also.

Sūryaḥ, saratīti, one who is constantly on the move. The Sun appears to go round the earth. Of course, it is the earth which is going round the Sun. But the Sun is not stationary. The Sun is moving in a straight line within the milky way galaxy. There is nothing stationary in this universe. It is also an expanding universe. The Vedas describe the universe as *brahmāṇḍa,* the expanding egg. The expansion of the universe was an unknown concept to the West till the first part of the twentieth century, when Hubble discovered that the universe continues to expand.

Khagaḥ, khe gacchati iti, one who moves in the universal space.

Pūṣā, puṣṇāti iti; one who provides food for all living beings. In some of these names, there is some repetition. As the one who gives birth to all life forms, the Sun is Savitā. The Sun is Pūṣā as the one who sustains the life forms after they are born.

Gabhastimān, one who has rays of light. The Sun radiates many types of rays, like visible radiation, ultra-violet rays, gamma rays, x-rays, cosmic rays (high speed protons), etc.

Suvarṇasadṛśaḥ, one who shines with brilliant golden yellow colour, while rising in the east.

Bhānuḥ, one who illuminates everything. In the tropical countries like India, the Sun is very brilliant. We dare not look at the afternoon Sun, particularly in the summer.

Hiraṇyaretāḥ. *Retas* means the seed, the seed of the universe. It entirely consists of *hiraṇya*, which is energy. In the *Taittirīya-Saṁhitā* (6-1-10) the word *hiraṇya* is defined as energy:

> तेजो वै हिरण्यम् ।
> *tejo vai hiraṇyam* ।
>
> Hiraṇyam is indeed the fire of energy.

Therefore, Hiraṇyaretas is the same as Hiraṇyagarbha, the progenitor of the universe, who is the single source of all energy of the universe. The Sun stands for that Cosmic Person. All life forms like plants and trees, insects and creatures, birds and animals, humans and angels, have their origin and existence in that Universal Person.

Divākaraḥ, the one who makes the day. The entire phenomenal world is dependent upon the concept of time, and its division into days and nights. This division is caused by the movement of the Sun relative to the earth.

[11]

हरिदश्वस्सहस्रार्चिस्सप्तसप्तिर्मरीचिमान् ।
तिमिरोन्मथनश्शम्भुस्त्वष्टा मार्तण्डकोऽशुमान् ।।

***haridaśvassahasrārcissaptasaptirmarīcimān* ।**
timironmathanaśśambhustvaṣṭā mārtaṇḍa-
***ko'ṁśumān* ॥**

हरिदश्वः (*haridaśvaḥ*) — one who pervades the quarters, सहस्रार्चिः (*sahasrācīḥ*) — one who has infinite rays, सप्तसप्तिः (*saptasaptiḥ*) — one who has seven horses, मरीचिमान् (*marīcimān*) — one who has many rays, तिमिरोन्मथनः (*timironmathanaḥ*) — one who dispels darkness, शम्भुः (*śambhuḥ*) — one who bestows happiness, त्वष्टा (*tvaṣṭā*) — one who eliminates suffering, मार्तण्डकः (*mārtaṇḍakaḥ*) — one who breathes life into the egg of the universe, अंशुमान् (*aṁśumān*) — one who has many rays.

The Sun, who shines brilliantly with infinite rays, pervades all the ten directions with his rays. The Sun, who is full of

> rays, has seven horses. He drives away the darkness. He is the source of all prosperity and happiness in life. He eliminates suffering from the lives of the devotees. With his rays He breathes life into an otherwise insentient egg of the universe.

Haridaśvaḥ, haritaḥ aśnoti iti, one who pervades the quarters with his rays.

Sahasrārciḥ, one who has infinite rays, pervading the entire solar system. The word *sahasra* means a thousand as well as infinite. Also, the *Brahman* abiding in the cave of the heart as Awareness, has infinite expressions in the form of thoughts.

Saptasaptiḥ, one who has seven horses. The Sun seems to travel a lot of distance in a given day, day after day, forever and without fail. He must have a chariot. If so, there must be horses to draw that chariot. Indeed the Vedas symbolically say that the chariot of the Sun is yoked to seven horses. This is beautifully narrated in the *Taittirīya Āraṇyaka* (3-11) as follows:

> सप्त युञ्जन्ति रथमेकचक्रम् । एक अश्वो वहति सप्तनामा । त्रिनाभि चक्रमजरमनर्वम् । येनेमे विश्वा भुवनानि तस्थुः ।।
>
> *sapta yuñjanti rathamekacakram* । *eka aśvo vahati saptanāmā* । *trinābhi cakramajaramanarvam* । *yeneme viśvā bhuvanāni tasthuḥ* ॥
>
> Seven horses draw the chariot of one wheel. It is indeed only one horse with seven different names. The wheel has three hubs. Nothing can destroy this immortal wheel. All life in this world exists because of those horses and that wheel.

The wheel is the cycle of time. The three hubs are the past, present, and the future. The seven horses are the seven rays of the spectrum of the composite visible light. It is interesting to note that the spectrum of visible light is recited in Vedic families by kids that are 8 to 10 years old clad in loin-cloth. The same spectrum was rediscovered later by Sir Isaac Newton in seventeenth century.

> आरोगो भ्राजः पटरः पतङ्गः। स्वर्णरो ज्योतिषीमान् विभासः। ते अस्मै सर्वे दिवमातपन्ति। ऊर्जं दुहाना अनपस्फुरन्त इति।।
>
> *ārogo bhrājaḥ paṭaraḥ pataṅgaḥ* । *svarṇaro jyotiṣīmān vibhāsaḥ* । *te asmai sarve divamātapanti* । *ūrjaṁ duhānā anapa-sphuranta iti* ॥ — *Ibid.*, 1-7
>
> Red, indigo, blue, green, yellow, orange, and violet are the seven rays of the Sun that reach this earth from the outer space, providing energy to all life forms, yet not causing any harm to them.

The composite nature of the sunlight, mentioned above metaphorically as the single horse, is clearly mentioned in the same section (1-3) of the *Taittirīya Āraṇyaka*.

> साकं जानां सप्तथमाहुरेकजम् ।
> *sākaṁ jānāṁ saptathamāhurekajam* ।
>
> The seven rays originate from a single composite ray.

Marīcimān, *timironmathanaḥ* and *aṁśumān* are different ways of describing the brilliance of the Sun.

Śambhuḥ, śam asmādbhavati iti. The Sun is the source of all comfort and happiness. It is of common experience that the rising Sun dispels our inertia, fills us with freshness and energy, and generally makes us happy. The rays of the morning Sun are not only soothing and comfortable to the body, but they also generate Vitamin D in the body, and make bones stronger. One *mantra* from the *Taittirīya-Saṁhitā* (1-4-23) is a prayer to the Sun as follows:

> वाममद्य सवितर्वाममु श्वो दिवे दिवे वाममस्मभ्यं सावीः ।
> *vāmamadya savitarvāmamu śvo dive dive vāmama-smabhyaṁ sāvīḥ* ।

> O Sun, bestow on us happiness today, tomorrow, and every-day hereafter.

Tvaṣṭā, one who alleviates the suffering of the devotees. Diseases have a way of causing all sorts of problems particularly at night. The moment the day breaks, the pain of illness fades away. This is our normal experience. For example, tooth ache is generally acute in the night, and is on the wane by morning. There seems to be a connection between the pain of illness and the night. That is why, a sick person looks forward to the daybreak. He thinks: 'If I can survive the pain through the night, I will be saved by the daybreak.' The Sun mitigates the pain of diseases through his rays.

Mārtaṇḍakaḥ, mṛtaṁ aṇḍaṁ jīvayati iti. Īśvara as the Sun breathes life into this universe. There is only one life in this creation and that is *Īśvara*. It is well known that all life on earth has its origin in the energy poured out by the Sun in the form of light and heat into the system of planets.

[12]

हिरण्यगर्भश्शिशिरस्तपनोऽहस्करो रविः ।
अग्निगर्भोऽदितेः पुत्रश्शङ्खश्शिशिरनाशनः ।।

hiraṇyagarbhaśśiśirastapano'haskaro raviḥ ।
agnigarbho'diteḥ putraśśaṅkhaśśiśira-nāśanaḥ ॥

हिरण्यगर्भः (*hiraṇyagarbhaḥ*) — the Cosmic Person, शिशिरः (*śiśiraḥ*) — one who gives comfort, तपनः (*tapanaḥ*) — one who causes discomfort due to excessive heat, अहस्करः (*ahaskaraḥ*) — one who brings the light of the dawn, रविः (*raviḥ*) — one who is praised by all, अग्निगर्भः (*agnigarbhaḥ*) — one who is all fire in the core, अदितेः पुत्रः (*aditeḥ putraḥ*) — the son of Aditi, शङ्खः (*śaṅkhaḥ*) — one whose nature is happiness unlimited, or one who pervades everything, शिशिरनाशनः (*śiśiranāśanaḥ*) — one who destroys cold.

> The Sun is the Cosmic Person. He causes comfort and also discomfort with his rays. He rises boisterously and brings forth the daybreak. He is all fire in the core. The Sun, the offspring of Aditi, is the all-pervading *Brahman* of infinite bliss. He casts off the cold.

Hiraṇyagarbhaḥ, hiraṇyaṁ garbhe yasya saḥ, one who has the Universal energy in Himself. As already mentioned, this description of the Lord is similar to the modern Big Bang theory in some aspects. The primordial ylem from which the universe was created was a dense ball of infinite energy. Its temperature is estimated to be 10^{10} degrees, which is beyond anybody's imagination. The energy in that ball was so immense that there was no difference between energy and mass; they merged into one. The particles like protons, neutrons, electrons did not exist in it. They are all latter products. According to modern theory of creation, even the difference between electro-magnetism and gravitation is obliterated inside that ultimate source of the Universe. The *Taittirīya Saṁhitā* (4-1-8) describes the creator thus:

> हिरण्यगर्भस्समवर्तताग्रे भूतस्य जातः पतिरेक आसीत् ।
> स दाधार पृथिवीं द्यामुतेमां कस्मै देवाय हविषा विधेम ।।
>
> *hiraṇyagarbhassamavartatāgre bhūtasya jātaḥ patireka āsīt* ।
> *sa dādhāra pṛthivīṁ dyāmutemāṁ kasmai devāya haviṣā vidhema* ॥
>
> Hiraṇyagarbha manifested (from *Brahman*) prior to the creation of this universe. He is the overlord of this universe, which was created out of Himself. He sustains the earth and other worlds of the universe. We worship that non-dual Godhead by offering oblations.

The main import of this encomium is that Hiraṇyagarbha, the Creator of this universe, manifests before us as the Sun.

Śiśiraḥ, comfortably warm. *Tapanaḥ,* its opposite, meaning, quite hot. These are the two aspects of the Sun in the morning and in the afternoon respectively.

Ahaskaraḥ, same as *divākaraḥ*. Yet there is a shade of difference between the two meanings. *Ahas* is a day. Even a cloudy day is a day. But, *divā* is a brilliant sunny day. You can have a great picnic on such a day.

Raviḥ, rauti iti; one who makes a loud sound. *Rava* is sound. In the *Chāndogyopaniṣat* (1-5-1), it is described that as the Sun moves, the sound of *om* emerges from that movement.

> ओमिति ह्येष स्वरन्नेति ।
> *omiti hyeṣa svaranneti* ।
>
> This Sun moves forward while making the sound *om*.

We are at a very long distance from the Sun; 8 × 60 × 86,000 miles to be precise, and the light from the Sun reaches the earth in eight minutes. Hence, we cannot hear the sound of the Sun's motion. Sun is also the teacher of the Vedas, the *Yajurveda* in particular. It is obvious that teaching of the Vedas involves the sound of speech, since the Vedas are learnt in the oral tradition of teaching.

Agnigarbhaḥ, agniḥ garbhe yasya saḥ. The core of the Sun is the most powerful source of all heat in this solar system. There, nuclear reactions equivalent to billions of hydrogen bombs are taking place every second. If it is said that an atom bomb serves as a trigger for the hydrogen bomb, the power of the latter can only be a matter of imagination at best. The Solar scientists say that the surface of the Sun is relatively cool when compared with the core of the Sun! If that is cool, then what hot could be!

Aditeḥ putraḥ, the offspring of Aditi, the Universal Power of *Īśvara*. Diti is *dvaita*, which is plurality. If we take the plurality that appears before us as the universe to be real, it is ignorance in the vision of the Vedas; and Diti stands for that ignorance. The offspring of Diti are *daityas*, who are the demons. They take the body to be the *ātmạn*, because they are the offspring of ignorance. Aditi stands for Oneness, which is the Reality. The plural can never be Real. Only Unity is

Real. Therefore, the offspring of Aditi (the Sun) stands for all knowledge, which is *Brahman*.

Śaṅkhaḥ, śam ca kham ca. Śam is Happiness and *kham* is space. *Kham* is also *Brahman*. The *Chāndogyopaniṣat* (4-10-4) presents this aspect of *Brahman* as follows:

> प्राणो ब्रह्म कं ब्रह्म खं ब्रह्मेति ।
> *prāṇo brahma kaṁ brahma khaṁ brahmeti* ।
>
> The Universal Power is *Brahman*, the happiness is *Brahman*, and the space (of awareness) is *Brahman*.

So, *śaṅkha* means the space of awareness, which is all happiness, and which is the Ultimate Reality.

Śiśiranāśanaḥ, śiśiram nāśayati iti. Śiśira is cold, or the dullness of the mind. The Sun destroys both. Worship of the Sun gives knowledge to the seeker.

[13]

व्योमनाथस्तमोभेदी ऋग्यजुस्सामपारगः ।
घनवृष्टिरपां मित्रो विन्ध्यवीथीप्लवङ्गमः ।।

vyomanāthastamobhedī ṛgyajussāmapāragaḥ ।
ghanavṛṣṭirapāṁ mitro vindhyavīthī-plavaṅgamaḥ ॥

व्योमनाथः (*vyomanāthaḥ*) — the Lord of the skies, तमोभेदी (*tamobhedī*) — the destroyer of darkness, ऋग्यजुस्सामपारगः (*ṛgyajussāmapāragaḥ*) — the supreme scholar of the *Ṛgveda*, the *Yajurveda* and the *Sāmaveda*, घनवृष्टिः (*ghanavṛṣṭiḥ*) — the cause of good rains, अपां मित्रः (*apāṁ mitraḥ*) — the friend or benefactor of waters, विन्ध्यवीथीप्लवङ्गमः (*vindyavīthī-plavaṅgamaḥ*) — one who moves very swiftly in the galactical space.

The Sun, who destroys the darkness, is the Lord of the skies.

> He is the greatest scholar of the *Ṛgveda*, the *Yajurveda* and the *Sāmaveda*. He is the friend of waters and water bodies, and so He gives copious rains. He moves swiftly in the galactical space.

Vyomanāthaḥ, the lord of the skies, the lord of the interstellar space; also, the progenitor of the space. Space is created along with galaxies from Hiraṇyagarbha. Also, in the scheme of creation as described in the *Taittirīyopaniṣat* (2-1), space is the very first product of *Brahman*.

> तस्माद्वा एतस्मादात्मन आकाशस्सम्भूतः। आकाशाद्वायुः। वायोरग्निः। अग्नेरापः।
>
> *tasmādvā etasmādātmana ākāśassambhūtaḥ* I *ākāśādvāyuḥ* I *vāyoragniḥ* I *agnerāpaḥ* II
>
> From this *Brahman*, which is *ātman*, there arose the space; from space the air was born; from air the fire; from the fire the waters.

Tamobhedī, one who destroys the *tamo-guṇa*. This *tamo-guṇa* expresses itself in us as the laziness of the physical body and dullness of the mind. Worship of the Sun removes both these problems.

Ṛgyajussāmapāragaḥ. In the Vedic tradition, the Sun is the first teacher. All knowledge was given to Him by the Lord at the time of creation (see verse 9). The Sun was the best student of *Īśvara*. *Īsvara* taught the Vedic knowledge consisting of *karma-yoga* and *jñāna-yoga*. The way the Sun conducts himself is the best example of *karma-yoga* as well as of *jñāna-yoga*. He performs his duty of creating life on earth, causing seasons, keeping the planets in their places, etc., without the two common errors of the sense of doership and the greed for the results of actions. Thus, He is a great *karma-yogī*. Also, while giving light and heat, the Sun does not differentiate among the recipients of His beneficience. He is *samadarśī*. Also, *Īśvara* in the form of the Sun is the ultimate reality described in all the Vedas.

Ghanavṛṣṭiḥ, ghanā vṛṣṭiḥ yasmāt saḥ. The Sun causes the evaporation of billions of gallons of water, performing like a giant pump from the seas. He holds all that water in the skies; and when time comes, all that water is released onto the earth.

Apāṁ mitraḥ, the friend of waters. The Sun is considered as the friend of waters. Why? The Sun is all fire, and waters are born from the fire (see above). Also, the Sun is the best friend for all the water bodies. He fills them with rain water. He transfers a lot of water from the ocean into the lakes and rivers, after purifying it from salts by the process of evaporation. The water bodies express their happiness and gratitude to the Sun through the croaks of the frogs.

Vindhyavīthīplavaṅgamaḥ. *Vindhyavīthī* is the interstellar space in which the Sun moves. He swiftly moves in that space.

[14]

आतपी मण्डली मृत्युः पिङ्गलस्सर्वतापनः।
कविर्विश्वो महातेजा रक्तस्सर्वभवोद्भवः ।।

***ātapī maṇḍalī mṛtyuḥ piṅgalassarvatāpanaḥ* ।**
***kavirviśvo mahātejā raktassarvabhavod-bhavaḥ* ॥**

आतपी (*ātapī*) — one who is hot, मण्डली (*maṇḍalī*) — repository of light, मृत्युः (*mṛtuḥ*) — the Lord of death, पिङ्गलः (*piṅgalaḥ*) — honey coloured, सर्वतापनः (*sarvatāpanaḥ*) — one who causes widespread discomfort due to excessive heat, कविः (*kaviḥ*) — the knower of the past, the present and the future, विश्वः (*viśvaḥ*) — the one who manifested as all, महातेजाः (*mahātejāḥ*) — the one who has great brilliance, रक्तः (*raktaḥ*) — red in hue, सर्वभवोद्भवः (*sarvabhavodbhavaḥ*) — the source of all creation.

The Sun, the burning orb of light and heat, is honey-coloured and red in hue while rising in the east. Later, He becomes very hot and brilliant and causes widespread discomfort with excessive heat. As the Lord of death, he knows the past, the present, and the future of all living beings. All creation has originated from Him. He alone manifests as all in this universe.

Ātapī, ā samantāt tāpaḥ asya asti iti, one who causes widespread sultriness and heat.

Maṇḍalī, a burning orb of light and energy. The Sun is the presiding deity of the burning orb. The solar orb is the *adhibhūta*, while the Sun is *adhidaiva*.

Mṛtyuḥ, the Lord of death. As described earlier, the Sun is regarded as the Lord of death. The *Taittirīya Āraṇyaka* (1-8-4) describes the Sun indeed as death.

> अमुमाहुः परं मृत्युम् ।
> *amumāhuḥ paraṁ mṛtyum* ।
>
> The Sun, seen yonder in the interstellar space, is the ultimate cause of death.

Piṅgalaḥ, honey-coloured in the morning only for a while.

Sarvatāpanaḥ, one who heats up and burns all. In the summer in tropics, all life forms suffer in the sweltering heat, as the Sun blazes overhead.

Kaviḥ, omniscient. *Īśvara* is described in the *Taittirīya Āraṇyaka* (10-11) as *kavi*, the omniscient:

> अनन्तमव्ययं कविम्।
> *anantamavyayaṁ kavim* ।
>
> The Lord is beyond the limitation of time, space, and objects. He is omniscient.

Viśvaḥ, one who manifested as this universe. The *Viṣṇusahasranāma* starts with the name *viśvam*. This universe which is a collection of different forms and names is called *viśva*. Its reality is not the names and forms, which are only apparent. Its reality is *Īśvara* alone, like even the reality of necklace is gold alone. The *Taittirīya Āraṇyaka* (10-11) describes as follows:

विश्वमेवेदं पुरुषः।
viśvamevedaṁ puruṣaḥ ।

This universe is indeed the Cosmic Person.

Also, every object, living and non-living, in this world, is a manifestation of solar energy alone. The names Mahātejāḥ, Raktaḥ, Sarvabhavodbhavaḥ are self-explanatory.

[15]

नक्षत्रग्रहताराणामधिपो विश्वभावनः।
तेजसामपि तेजस्वी द्वादशात्मन्नमोऽस्तु ते।।

nakṣatragrahatārāṇāmadhipo viśvabhāvanaḥ ।
tejasāmapi tejasvī dvādaśātmannamo'stu te ॥

नक्षत्रग्रहताराणाम् (*nakṣatragrahatārāṇām*) — of the stars of different types and the planets, अधिपः (*adhipaḥ*) — the overlord, विश्वभावनः (*viśvabhāvanaḥ*) — the originator of the universe, तेजसां अपि (*tejasāṁ api*) — among all luminous celestial bodies, तेजस्वी (*tejasvī*) — the most luminous, द्वादशात्मन् (*dvādaśātman*) — one who manifested in twelve forms, ते (*te*) — unto you, नमः अस्तु (*namaḥ astu*) — prostration.

The Sun is the overlord of the planets and different types of stars. The Sun, who is the most brilliant of all the luminous bodies, is the originator and sustainer of the universe. He manifests himself in twelves forms. My prostrations unto Him.

Nakṣatragrahatārāṇāmadhipaḥ. The Sun is the foremost of all the luminous bodies in the sky. There are many stars that are even bigger and more brilliant than the Sun. But, from the point of view of an observer on the earth, the Sun is the most brilliant of all. So, we say that the Sun is the king of stars. He is obviously the king of all planets.

Viśvabhāvanaḥ, the creator and protector of the universe. The Sun stands for *Īśvara*, the creator and protector.

Tejasāmapi tejasvī. In the entire universe, there are many luminous bodies. From our point of view, the Sun is the most luminous of them all.

Dvādaśātman namo'stu te, O Sun of twelve forms, my prostrations unto you. The Sun enters a new house in the zodiac once every month. The Sun has a different character and a different name in everyone of these houses. Viṣṇu, Śakra, Aryamā, Dhātā, Tvaṣṭā, Pūṣā, Vivasvān, Savitā, Mitra, Varuṇa, Aṁśa and Bhaga are the twelve names of the Sun in His twelve forms.

[16]

नमः पूर्वाय गिरये पश्चिमायाद्रये नमः।
ज्योतिर्गणानां पतये दिनाधिपतये नमः।।

***namaḥ pūrvāya giraye paścimāyādraye namaḥ* |**
***jyotirgaṇānāṁ pataye dināadhipataye namaḥ* ||**

पूर्वाय गिरये (*pūrvāya giraye*) — unto the mountain in the east, पश्चिमाय अद्रये (*paścimāya adraye*) — unto the mountain in the west, ज्योतिर्गणानां (*jyotirgaṇānāṁ*) — of groups of luminous bodies, पतये (*pataye*) — unto the overlord, दिनाधिपतये (*dinādhipataye*) — unto the Lord of the day, नमः (*namaḥ*) — salutation.

My prostrations unto the eastern mountain on which the Sun rises, and also unto the western one where the Sun sets. My prostrations unto the Sun, who is the overlord of the day. He is the king of all the groups of luminous bodies in the sky.

The mountain range in the east appears to be the abode of the Sun, as He rises there in the morning. In the evening, as the Sun sets on the western mountain range, it appears to be His abode. The practitioner of Vedic culture offers oblation of water (*arghya*) to the Sun on both the occasions. The Sun is the readily available altar of worship. One does not need any other altar. Seekers worship the

Sun both in the morning and evening, particularly during the intervals between the setting of the Moon and the rising of the Sun, and vice versa. These intervals last around thirty minutes, and that period is very auspicious to worship the Lord. During that interval, the mind is naturally calm. Vedas describe the Sun as *atithi,* the beloved guest. We should welcome the guest as he appears on the horizon, and we should bid him farewell as he disappears beyond the horizon. We should pay our obeisance to this guest, who gives us life, nay everything.

Dinādhipataye namaḥ, prostrations unto the Lord of the day. While we are busily engaged in different chores during the daytime, we should always keep in the back of the mind that the Lord is always around us in the form of sunlight. We should always be sensitive to the presence of the Lord everywhere. We are able to function because of the grace and brilliance of the Sun alone. We should engage ourselves in different activities of the world with such an attitude of prayer.

[17]

जयाय जयभद्राय हर्यश्वाय नमो नमः।
नमो नमस्सहस्रांशो आदित्याय नमो नमः।।

jayāya jayabhadrāya haryaśvāya namo namaḥ **।**
namo namassahasrāṁśo ādityāya namo namaḥ **॥**

जयाय (*jayāya*) — unto one who is in the form of victory, जयभद्राय (*jayabhadrāya*) — unto one who is in the form of victory and auspicousness, हर्यश्वाय (*haryaśvāya*) — unto the one who pervades the quarters with his rays, सहस्रांशो (*sahasrāṁśo*) — O Lord of infinite rays, आदित्याय (*ādityāya*) — unto the Lord Āditya, नमः नमः (*namaḥ namaḥ*) — many salutations.

I salute any number of times the Lord Āditya who confers

auspicious victories on the devotees. He pervades the quarters with his infinite rays.

Jayāya. Prostrations unto the One who gives success in our endeavours. Earlier we had the names in first case (*prathamā vibhakti*). Now we have them in the fourth case (*caturthī vibhakti*). For the purpose of worship in the form of offering flowers, etc., all the names have to be changed into the fourth case, preceded by *om*, and followed by *namaḥ*. (A list of 125 such names is appended.)

Jayabhadrāya. He gives not only victory, but also auspiciousness; a victory which is auspicious.

Haryaśva is synonymous with *Haridaśva. Na me iti namaḥ*; in this creation, nothing is really mine. O Lord! Everything is given by you. I happen to possess a few things entirely because of your grace. I recognise that fact, and in the wake of that recognition, I surrender 'me' and 'mine' before you. That is the meaning of *namaḥ*. The sense of ownership, doership, and enjoyership is deeply ingrained in us. So, we may say *namaḥ* any number of times.

Namo namassahasrāṁśo; sahasraṁ anantāḥ aṁśavaḥ aṁśāḥ jīvāḥ yasya saḥ. Prostrations unto the Lord of infinite rays. Each *jīva* is a ray. The Lord says so in the *Gītā* (15-7):

> ममैवांशो जीवलोके जीवभूतस्सनातनः।
> *mamaivāṁśo jīvaloke jīvabhūtassanātanaḥ* ।
>
> The eternal *jīva*, appearing as an individual in the world of life forms, is indeed a part of Me alone.

[18]

नम उग्राय वीराय सारङ्गाय नमो नमः।
नमः पद्मप्रबोधाय प्रचण्डाय नमोऽस्तु ते।।

***nama ugrāya vīrāya sāraṅgāya namo namaḥ* ।**
***namaḥ padmaprabodhāya pracaṇḍāya namo'stu te* ।।**

उग्राय (*ugrāya*) — unto the one who is ferocious, वीराय (*vīrāya*) — unto the one who is powerful, सारङ्गाय (*sāraṅgāya*) — unto the one who moves swiftly, पद्मप्रबोधाय (*padmaprabodhāya*) — unto the one who causes the lotuses to blossom, प्रचण्डाय (*pracaṇḍāya*) — unto the one who is unbearable, ते (*te*) — unto You, नमः (*namaḥ*) — prostration.

I salute again and again the unbearably ferocious and powerful Sun, who traverses the skies swiftly, causing the lotuses to blossom.

Ugrāya, very ferocious. The Lord in the form of Rudra is called Ugra (*Rudrādhyāya*, 8) and the Sun is a manifestation of that Rudra.

Sāraṅgāya namo namaḥ, prostrations unto the One who traverses the interstellar space very swiftly. Also, *sāram* is *oṁkāra*, because it is the essence of all the Vedas. *Om* is the single most important syllable in Hindu culture. The Lord is realised in the heart by meditating on *om*.

Namaḥ padmaprabodhāya; prostrations unto the One who makes the lotuses blossom. Poets describe that the Sun and the lotus are the best of friends! The Sun as *ātman* also causes the heart of the devotee (often compared with a lotus) shine with consciousness. Padmā also means wealth. The Goddess of wealth, Lakṣmī, is also called Padmā, since lotus happens to be her abode. The Sun blesses the devotee with prosperity. The Lady Luck smiles on the devotee by the grace of the Lord Sun.

Pracaṇḍāya namo'stu te; O Lord! You are very ferocious; my prostrations unto you. It is very difficult to bear the intense heat of the summer Sun. What can we do, except offer prayers from a distance!

[19]

ब्रह्मेशानाच्युतेशाय सूरायादित्यवर्चसे।
भास्वते सर्वभक्षाय रौद्राय वपुषे नमः।।

brahmeśānācyuteśāya sūrāyādityavarcase ।

bhāsvate sarvabhakṣāya raudrāya vapuṣe namaḥ ॥

ब्रह्मेशानाच्युतेशाय (*brahmeśānācyuteśāya*) — unto the Lord even of the creator, sustainer and annihilator, सूराय (*sūrāya*) — unto the one who traverses the sky, आदित्यवर्चसे (*ādityavarcase*) — unto the one who shines brilliantly in the solar orb, भास्वते (*bhāsvate*) — unto the one who has all the brilliance, सर्वभक्षाय (*sarvabhakṣāya*) — unto the one who devours all, रौद्राय वपुषे (*raudrāya vpuṣe*) — unto the ferocious form, नमः (*namaḥ*) — salutations.

My salutations unto the *para-Brahman*, who is the Lord even of the creator, sustainer and annihilator, and who shines as the Sun in the solar orb. He is also in the form of the ferocious fire, which devours all.

Brahmeśānācyuteśāya. Brahmājī, the creator, Viṣṇu, the sustainer and Rudra, the annihilator are three aspects of the same Lord; who is shining before us in the form of the Sun, accomplishing all the three functions in this world by his rays as indeed pointed out by the *Taittirīya Āraṇyaka* (2-2):

> उद्यन्तमस्तं यन्तमादित्यमभिध्यायन् कुर्वन् ब्राह्मणो विद्वान् सकलं भद्रमश्नुतेऽसावादित्यो ब्रह्मेति।
>
> *udyantamastaṁ yantamādityamabhidhyāyan kurvan brāhmaṇo vidvān sakalaṁ bhadramaśnute'sāvādityo brahmeti* ।
>
> A scholar of Vedas, who meditates upon the Sun as the *para-Brahman*, as He rises and sets, gains all that is good. This Sun is indeed the *para-Brahman.*

Sūra is same as Sūrya. *Bhāsvate;* salutations to the One who is full of brilliance. *Bhā* also means knowledge. *Bhāsvān* is the Omniscient Lord.

Sarvabhakṣāya; salutation unto the One who devours everything. The *para-Brahman* is described in the *Kaṭhopaniṣat* (1-2-25) as *attā,* one who devours everything.

यस्य ब्रह्म च क्षत्रं चोभे भवत ओदनः।
मृत्युर्यस्योपसेचनं क इत्था वेद यत्र सः।।

yasya brahma ca kṣatraṁ cobhe bhavata odanaḥ ।
mṛtyuryasyopasecanaṁ ka itthā veda yatra saḥ ॥

The intellectual and the ruling class are the food and the god of death is the vegetable dressing for the *ātman*. Except for a highly qualified seeker, who can know its location?

Raudrāya vapuṣe namaḥ. At the time of annihilation, the Lord appears as a ferocious fire and devours everything. Also, the Lord who dispels the sorrow of the devotees is called Rudra (*rujam drāvayati iti*). This solar orb is a manifestation of that Lord.

[20]

तमोघ्नाय हिमघ्नाय शत्रुघ्नायामितात्मने।
कृतघ्नघ्नाय देवाय ज्योतिषां पतये नमः।।

tamoghnāya himaghnāya śatrughnāyāmit-ātmane ।
kṛtaghnaghnāya devāya jyotiṣām pataye namaḥ ॥

तमोघ्नाय (*tamoghnāya*) — unto the one who dispels darkness, हिमघ्नाय (*himaghnāya*) — unto the one who removes cold, शत्रुघ्नाय (*śatrughnāya*) — unto the one who destroys the enemies, अमितात्मने (*amitātmane*) — unto the one whose essential nature is beyond all limitations, कृतघ्नघ्नाय (*kṛtaghnaghnāya*) — unto the one who punishes the ungrateful, देवाय (*devāya*) — unto the Lord, ज्योतिषां (*jyotiṣāṁ*) — of the luminous bodies, पतये (*pataye*) — unto the overlord, नमः (*namaḥ*) — salutation.

My salutations unto the Lord, who dispels darkness, who removes the cold, who destroys the enemies, and who punishes the ungrateful. He is essentially beyond all limitations. He is the Lord of all luminous bodies.

Śatrughnāya, my salutations unto the Lord who destroys the enemies. The negative emotions, ill health, burden of debt, etc., are all considered as enemies, since they hinder the spiritual progress of the seeker.

Amitātmane, amitaḥ ātmā svarūpam yasya saḥ. Salutation unto the One whose nature is beyond the limitations of time and space. The size of the solar orb is 30,000 times greater than all the nine planets put together. This is an unimaginably huge, yet a finite size. Also, the solar orb has a beginning, as it came into being at the time of creation of the universe. But, the Cosmic Person as the presiding deity of the solar orb is eternal. As the originator of both time and space, He is beyond both time and space.

Kṛtaghnaghnāya, prostrations unto the One who destroys the ungrateful. These are the people who fail to recognise the service rendered to them by others, or even by the Lord. The Lord punishes such people. In Hindu scriptures, the gratitude shown for the help received is considered to be a very important virtue. Vālmīki describes Rāma as a role model of this virtue.

[21]

तप्तचामीकराभाय हरये विश्वकर्मणे।
नमस्तमोऽभिनिघ्नाय रुचये लोकसाक्षिणे।।

taptacāmīkarābhāya haraye viśvakarmaṇe ।
namastamo'bhinighnāya rucaye lokasākṣiṇe ॥

नमः (*namaḥ*) — salutation, तप्तचामीकराभाय (*taptacāmī-karābhāya*) — unto the one shining like pure gold, हरये (*haraye*) — destroyer of suffering, विश्वकर्मणे (*viśvakarmaṇe*) — unto the creator of the universe, तमोऽभिनिघ्नाय (*tamo'bhinighnāya*) — unto the destroyer of darkness, रुचये (*rucaye*) — unto the one who is shining, लोकसाक्षिणे (*lokasākṣiṇe*) — unto the witness of the world.

My salutations unto the Lord Sun, who shines like pure gold. He, the creator and witness of this universe, destroys the darkness and sufferings of the seekers.

Haraye, harati iti. The words *hariḥ, haraḥ, hrīṁ* and *hṛt* are all derived from the same verbal root *hriñ*, and they all mean the same, namely, *Īśvara*. The Lord is called Hari because he destroys the sins and eliminates the darkness of ignorance from the hearts of the devotees.

Viśvakarmaṇe, viśvam karma yasya. This universe is the handiwork of the Lord. All the activities in the world, big and small — an ant crawling, a person running, a big crane lifting loads, etc. — owe their origin directly or indirectly to the Lord Sun. But for the Sun, nothing would move in this world.

Lokasākṣiṇe, unto the eternal witness of the world. People commit prohibited acts like theft, and congratulate themselves that nobody has seen them in the act. But the Lord Sun is ever there as a witness. This is a beautiful vision of the Vedic sages. The *Taittirīya Saṁhitā* (3-4-11) describes the Lord Sun as follows:

> हिरण्ययेन सविता रथेना देवो याति भुवना विपश्यन्।
> *hiraṇyayena savitā rathenā devo yāti bhuvanā vipaśyan* ।
>
> The Lord in the form of the Sun traverses the skies with a golden chariot (the brilliant rays of light), while witnessing all the activities of the world.

[22]

नाशयत्येष वै भूतं तमेव सृजति प्रभुः।
पायत्येष तपत्येष वर्षत्येष गभस्तिभिः।।

nāśayatyeṣa vai bhūtaṁ tameva sṛjati prabhuḥ ।
pāyatyeṣa tapatyeṣa varṣatyeṣa gabhastibhiḥ ॥

एषः (*eṣaḥ*) — this, प्रभुः (*prabhuḥ*) — Lord, भूतम् (*bhūtam*) — the universe, वै (*vai*) — indeed, नाशयति (*nāśayati*) — destroys, तं एव (*taṁ eva*) — that again, सृजति (*sṛjati*) — creates, एषः (*eṣaḥ*) — this Lord, पायति (*pāyati*) — protects, एषः (*eṣaḥ*) — this Lord, गभस्तिभिः (*gabhastibhiḥ*) — with the rays, तपति (*tapati*) — heats up, एषः (*eṣaḥ*) — this Lord, वर्षति (*varṣati*) — rains.

> The Lord, as the Sun, creates this Universe, protects it, and finally annihilates it (into Himself). He heats up the world with his rays and thus causes rain.

Īśvara, who shines before us as the Sun, creates the entire universe; He also destroys it. The Sun becomes cold at the time of annihilation, and that will be the end of all life. Between the creation and destruction, He protects the universe.

He blazes in the summer, and He gives plenty of water again in the form of rain later. He accomplishes all this with his rays. In the *Gītā* (9-19), *Bhagavān* declares thus:

> तपाम्यहमहं वृष्टिं निगृह्णाम्युत्सृजामि च।
> *tapāmyahamahaṁ vr̥ṣṭiṁ nigr̥hṇāmyutsr̥jāmi ca* ।
>
> I cause suffering due to excessive heat. I cause severe evaporation of water (from the water bodies), and then I also cause the downpour of water (in the form of rain).

[23]

एष सुप्तेषु जागर्ति भूतेषु परिनिष्ठितः।
एष चैवाग्निहोत्रं च फलं चैवाग्निहोत्रिणाम्।।

***eṣa supteśu jāgarti bhūteṣu pariniṣṭhitaḥ* ।**
***eṣa caivāgnihotraṁ ca phalaṁ caivāgni-hotriṇām* ॥**

एषः (*eṣaḥ*) — This Sun, भूतेषु (*bhūteṣu*) — as the living beings, सुप्तेषु (*supteṣu*) — while fast asleep, परिनिष्ठितः (*pariniṣṭhitaḥ*) — abiding as the inner vitality, जागर्ति (*jāgarti*) — keeps awake, एषः एव (*eṣaḥ eva*) — this Lord alone, अग्निहोत्रम् (*agnihotram*) — the Vedic ritual, च (*ca*) — and, अग्निहोत्रिणाम् (*agnihotriṇām*) — of the performers of the Vedic rituals, फलम् (*phalam*) — result.

This Sun, abiding in all the living beings as the inner vitality, keeps awake while all of them are fast asleep. He is in the form of the Vedic rituals performed by the Vaidikas. He is also in the form of the results thereof.

The Sun, abiding in his own orb as the presiding deity, is shining ever, even while all the life on earth goes to sleep after the apparent sunset. It is obvious that while there is a day and night from the point of view of the person standing on earth, the Sun Himself is utterly devoid of any such distinction. To put it poetically, there is no sleep for Him. He always shines.

Also, the same Lord, who shines in the solar orb, abides in the hearts of the living beings as the inner sentience called *antaryāmī*. As the *ātman*, the ultimate Reality, He is ever awake (shining) in the beings while they are asleep. The *Kaṭhopaniṣat* (2-2-8) also describes *Īśvara* in similar terms:

> एष सुप्तेषु जागर्ति कामं कामं पुरषो निर्मिमाणः।
> तदेव शुक्रं तद्ब्रह्म तदेवामृतमुच्यते।।
>
> *eṣa supteṣu jāgarti kāmaṁ kāmaṁ puruṣo nirmimāṇaḥ* ।
> *tadeva śukraṁ tadbrahma tadevāmṛtamucyate* ॥
>
> This *ātman*, abiding in the living beings as the Awareness, is beyond the limitations of time and space. While the organs of action and the sense-organs are asleep, this *ātman* keeps awake illuminating the dream projected by the mind — the dream consisting of all the things desired. It is said by the learned that this *ātman*, unsullied by these states of mind, is indeed the immortal *Brahman*.

Sleep is not void. It is obvious that all the functions of life are active in the sleep state also. *Ātman*, the Awareness, is ever present in all three states of experience, namely, waking, dream and sleep. Sleep is an experience of the relative absence of everything that appears in the waking state. That is the reason why everybody asserts that he had slept well without knowing anything around him. That sentience which is ever awake and active is an expression of the Infinite in the finite body. *Bhagavān* says in the *Gītā* (18-61):

ईश्वरस्सर्वभूतानां हृद्देशेऽर्जुन तिष्ठति।
Īśvarassarvabhūtānāṁ hṛddeśe'rjuna tiṣṭhati ।

O Arjuna, the Lord abides in the cave of heart of all living beings.

Eṣa caivāgnihotraṁ ca. He is the fire altar worshipped by the Vaidikas. Even the ritual of offering oblations in the fire is the Lord Viṣṇu, in the form of the Sun, as declared in the *Taittirīya Saṁhitā* (2-5-5):

यज्ञो वै विष्णुः।
yajño vai viṣṇu ।

The Vedic ritual is indeed Lord Viṣṇu.

Phalaṁ caivāgnihotriṇām. He bestows the results of actions upon the individuals. The Vaidika, who performs the fire ritual, is bestowed upon with the heavens after his death by the Lord. *Brahman* alone manifested as this universe. Therefore, that heaven is not different from *Brahman*. Also, *Bhagavān* gives *mokṣa* (liberation) to the seekers of Self-knowledge and that *mokṣa* is not different from Him either. *Bhagavān* declares in the *Gītā* (7-18):

ज्ञानी त्वात्मैव मे मतम् ।
jñānī tvātmaiva me matam ।
It is my considered opinion that the knower of the Self is indeed Me.

[24]

देवाश्च क्रतवश्चैव क्रतूनां फलमेव च।
यानि कृत्यानि लोकेषु सर्वेषु परमप्रभुः।।

***devāśca kratavaścaiva kratūnāṁ phalamev ca* ।**
***yāni kṛtyāni lokeṣu sarveṣu paramaprabhuḥ* ॥**

देवाः (*devāḥ*) — the gods, क्रतवः (*kratavaḥ*) — Vedic rituals, एव (*eva*) — indeed, क्रतूनाम् (*kratūṇām*) — of those Vedic rituals, फलमेव च (*phalameva ca*) — even the result also, सर्वेषु (*sarveṣu*) — all, लोकेषु (*lokeṣu*) — worlds, यानि (*yāni*) — whichever, कृत्यानि (*kṛtyāni*) — activities, परमप्रभुः (*paramaprabhuḥ*) — omnipotent.

The Sun alone manifests as the gods, as the Vedic rituals, and even as their results. The Omnipotent Lord alone expresses Himself in all the activities of all the life forms of all the worlds.

All the gods — Indra, Varuṇa, Agni, Soma, etc. who receive the oblations offered in the Vedic rituals — are so many limbs of that Cosmic Person. Sense-organs are also called *deva*s. The power of knowing is bestowed on them by the Lord Himself, who is the *ātman*. All *pūjā*s, all offerings or oblations in the fire, various rituals such as *agniṣṭoma, āptoryāma, vājapeya, caṇḍīyāga, rudrayāga, atirudrayāga*, etc., are all made possible by the grace of the Lord in the form of the Sun. The results of all these rituals, like prosperity in this world, heaven after death, etc., are bestowed upon the deserving by the Lord Himself.

Also, the motive power of all living beings in this world is due to the grace of the Lord Sun. Even the slightest movement is made possible by the energy given by the Sun. Thus, the Sun is the Supreme Overlord of all life and all activities on the globe. All activity in all the worlds is nothing but the expression of the Infinite Power of the Lord Hiraṇyagarbha.

[25]

एनमापत्सु कृच्छ्रेषु कान्तारेषु भयेषु च।
कीर्तयन् पुरुषः कश्चिन्नावसीदति राघव।।

***enamāpatsu kṛcchreṣu kāntāreṣu bhayeṣu ca* ।**
***kīrtayan puruṣaḥ kaścinnāvasīdati rāghava* ॥**

राघव (*rāghava*) — O Rāma, आपत्सु (*āpatsu*) — in calamities, कृच्छ्रेषु (*kṛcchreṣu*) — in adverse situations, कान्तारेषु (*kāntāreṣu*) — in difficult paths, च (*ca*) — and, भयेषु (*bhayeṣu*) — in fears, एनम् (*enam*) — this Sun, कीर्तयन् (*kīrtayan*) — one who sings the glory, पुरुषः (*puruṣaḥ*) — person, कश्चित् (*kaścit*) — whosoever, न अवसीदति (*na avasīdati*) — does not get destroyed.

O Rāma, whosoever sings the glory of this Sun (through this encomium) will not come to grief, even if such a person finds himself in calamities, dire straits, difficult paths or such other frightening situations.

O Rāghava, O Rāma of the clan of Raghu, a person who finds himself in adversitites or in very difficult situations, is advised to recite this encomium. He will be rescued from his difficulties. A person who lost his way in a forest or in the forest of life may recite these verses. People who lose their way in a forest are in deep trouble, because they cannot make out the direction in which they are moving. All directions look alike in a deep forest, deep seas and deep space. Figuratively, human life, with all the conflicting interests, is itself a forest. A person may find himself helpless in the face of the challenges posed by the life. In all such situations, the devotees are advised to recite *Āditya-Hṛdayam*. It will attract the grace of *Īśvara*, and will show the way out. Also, people suffer from all kinds of worries and fears. When one is alone in the house, even a little creaking sound could be a source of fear. There is then the fear of the adversary, as in the case of Rāma. Under all such circumstances, one who recites these verses will not come to grief. His life and his goals will be taken care of by the grace of *Īśvara*.

[26]

पूजयस्वैनमेकाग्रो देवदेवं जगत्पतिम् ।
एतत् त्रिगुणितं जप्त्वा युद्धेषु विजयिष्यति ।।

pūjayasvainamekāgro devadevaṁ jagatpatim ।
etat triguṇitaṁ japtvā yuddheṣu vijayiṣyati ॥

देवदेवम् (*devadevam*) — the Lord of the lords, जगत्पतिम् (*jagatpatim*) — the Overlord of the universe, एनम् (*enam*) — this Sun, एकाग्रः (*ekāgraḥ*) — having a single-pointed mind, पूजयस्व (*pūjayasva*) — worship, एतत् (*etat*) — this, त्रिगुणितम् (*triguṇitam*) — three times, जप्त्वा (*japtvā*) — having recited, युद्धेषु (*yuddheṣu*) — in the battles, विजयिष्यति (*vijayiṣyati*) — will win.

This Sun is the Lord of the lords and the Overlord of the universe. Worship Him with a single-pointed mind. One will secure victory in the battles by reciting these verses thrice.

One may recite this *stotra* thrice when one is faced with exceptional difficulties. During the normal course, one may recite it once. But, the important point is that one may not recite it mechanically. We have to recite it by focusing the mind, to the extent possible, on the profound meaning of the verses. That was the advice of Agastya to Rāma. This *stotra* will give victory to the devotee in all the righteous pursuits.

[27]

अस्मिन् क्षणे महाबाहो रावणं त्वं जहिष्यसि।
एवमुक्त्वा ततोऽगस्त्यो जगाम स यथागतम् ।।

asmin kṣaṇe mahābāho rāvaṇaṁ tvaṁ jahiṣyasi ।
evamuktvā tato'gastyo jagāma sa yathāgatam ॥

महाबाहो (*mahābāho*) — O mighty armed, त्वम् (*tvam*) — you, अस्मिन् (*asmin*) — in this, क्षणे (*kṣaṇe*) — moment, रावणम् (*rāvaṇam*) — Rāvaṇa, जहिष्यसि (*jahiṣyasi*) — shall slay, एवम् (*evam*) — thus, उक्त्वा (*uktvā*) — having spoken, ततः (*tataḥ*) — then, सः (*saḥ*) — that, अगस्त्यः (*agastyaḥ*) — Agastya, यथागतम् (*yathāgatam*) — the way he came, जगाम (*jagāma*) — went.

O mighty armed Rāma, you are going to slay Rāvaṇa this very moment. Having spoken thus, that sage Agastya went the way he came.

Agastya assures Rāma that Rāvaṇa's day of doom is at hand. So, Rāma may not worry or hesitate. Victory is certain. Victory would come to Rāma immediately after reciting this *stotra*. Similar results are bound to occur to us too. Having done his job, Agastya went his way. He did not wait around to be rewarded or even to be thanked. He is a liberated soul; he has no other agenda. He wanted Rāma to win. In fact, the gods requested Agastya to secure victory for Rāma. One should not think that this narration reduces the importance of Lord Rāma. Vālmīki presented Rāma as the greatest of the human beings, who stood upright in the face of direst adversity, and who protected *dharma* and retained his own character. In receiving this *stotra* from a great sage and then following his advice by reciting it, Rāma presents a wonderful example before the entire mankind.

[28]

एतच्छ्रुत्वा महातेजा नष्टशोकोऽभवत्तदा।
धारयामास सुप्रीतो राघवः प्रयतात्मवान्।।

***etacchrutvā mahātejā naṣṭaśoko'bhavattadā* |**
***dhārayāmāsa suprīto rāghavaḥ prayat-ātmavān* ||**

तदा (*tadā*) — then, महातेजाः (*mahātejāḥ*) — very brilliant and powerful, राघवः (*rāghavaḥ*) — Rāma, the scion of Raghu clan, एतत् (*etat*) — this, श्रुत्वा (*śrutvā*) — having heard, नष्टशोकः (*naṣṭaśokaḥ*) one whose affliction is destroyed, अभवत् (*abhavat*) — became, सुप्रीतः (*suprītaḥ*) — very much pleased, प्रयतात्मवान् (*prayatātmavān*) — one who has perfect self-control, धारयामास (*dhārayāmāsa*) — memorised or held on to.

Then Rāma, the scion of the Raghu clan, received the advice of Agastya. His affliction was at once cast off. He was very happy. Being a man of perfect self-control, he memorised it and held on to that encomium.

Rāma is potentially a great warrior. He needed this encouragement from Agastya to manifest that innate potential in the battlefield. Recitation of this *stotra* removed his gloom. He regained all his enthusiasm. He now had no doubt about victory. This encomium is a morale booster. Rāma immediately knew it by heart. He could commit anything to memory just by reciting once. That speaks volumes about his self-control, since it is not easy to concentrate the mind on an encomium right in the middle of the battlefield.

[29]

आदित्यं प्रेक्ष्य जप्त्वेदं परं हर्षमवाप्तवान्।
त्रिराचम्य शुचिर्भूत्वा धनुरादाय वीर्यवान्।।

***ādityaṁ prekṣya japtvedaṁ paraṁ harṣama-
vāptavān |
trirācamya śucirbhūtvā dhanurādāya vīrya-
vān ||***

वीर्यवान् (*vīryavān*) — Rāma, the warrior of prowess, त्रिः (*triḥ*) — thrice, आचम्य (*ācamya*) — having sipped water, शुचिः (*śuciḥ*) — pure, भूत्वा (*bhūtvā*) — having become, आदित्यम् (*ādityam*) — the Sun, प्रेक्ष्य (*prekṣya*) — having seen, इदम् (*idam*) — this encomium, जप्त्वा (*japtvā*) — having recited, धनुः (*dhanuḥ*) — bow, आदाय (*ādāya*) — having taken, परम् (*param*) — immense, हर्षम् (*harṣam*) — joy, अवाप्तवान् (*avāptavān*) — gained.

Rāma, the warrior of prowess, sipped water thrice and thus purified himself. Then he looked at the Sun and recited this encomium and became immensely joyous. Then he took the bow into the hand.

Sipping water three times imparts purity to the body as well as mind. When there is no facility to take bath, this practice could be very useful. Even looking at the Sun with devotion purifies and rejuvenates a person. Nowadays, even cricket players from India first display their devotion to the Sun. That is very nice to see. In Indian villages, every farmer prays to the Sun first thing in the morning, after washing the face.

Recitation of this *stotra* delivers an immediate result. There will be an unseen future result too. One has to wait for it. The mechanical nature of modern life makes the mind very agitated and restless. Practice of recitation certainly helps to overcome the stress. *Rāma* at once became very happy after the recitation. He is yet to kill Rāvaṇa and regain his beloved Sītā. In spite of it, and in the midst of a crisis, the prayer gave him happiness. He took the bow into the hand. He was ready for the battle. This is the immediate result of reciting the *stotra* with devotion.

Worship the Sun for ten minutes in the morning; then have breakfast and go to the waiting world like a hero!

[30]

रावणं प्रेक्ष्य हृष्टात्मा जयार्थं समुपागमत्।
सर्वयत्नेन महता वृतस्तस्य वधेऽभवत् ।।

***rāvaṇaṁ prekṣya hṛṣṭātmā jayārthaṁ samup-
āgamat* ।**
***sarvayatnena mahatā vṛtastasya vadhe-
'bhavat* ॥**

रावणम् (*rāvaṇam*) — Rāvaṇa, प्रेक्ष्य (*prakṣya*) — having seen, हृष्टात्मा (*hṛṣṭātmā*) — filled in the heart with joy, जयार्थम् (*jayārtham*) — for the sake of victory, समुपागमत् (*samupāgamat*) — proceeded forward, तस्य (*tasya*) — of him, वधे (*vadhe*) — in the slaying, महता (*mahatā*) — great, सर्वयत्नेन (*sarvayatnena*) — with an all-round effort, वृतः (*vṛtaḥ*) — ready, अभवत् (*abhavat*) — became.

Rāma looked at Rāvaṇa, and his heart was filled with joy. He proceeded forward to gain victory. He was ready to make a great all-round effort to slay Rāvaṇa.

Earlier he saw Rāvaṇa and became dejected. 'My god! I have to kill this person, a great warrior. Will I be able to do that?'. Those were Rāma's thoughts, but that crisis of confidence is no longer there. The whole situation had changed. As he saw Rāvaṇa again, he became confident that he can defeat him. He was determined to put in all the necessary effort to secure the victory. Prayer can bring about such a dramatic change in the mind. One has to first win the battle against oneself before fighting the situation outside. Therein lies the secret of *Āditya-Hṛdayam.*

[31]

अथ रविरवदन्निरीक्ष्य रामं मुदितमनाः परमं प्रहृष्यमाणः।
निशिचरपतिसंक्षयं विदित्वा सुरगणमध्यगतो वचस्त्वरेति।।

***atha raviravadannirīkṣya rāmaṁ muditamanāḥ
paramaṁ prahṛyamāṇaḥ* ।**

***niśicarapatisaṅkṣayaṁ viditvā suragaṇa-madhyagato vacastvareti* ॥**

अथ (*atha*) — Afterwards, सुरगणमध्यगतः (*suragaṇamadhyagataḥ*) — one who is in the midst of the groups of gods, रविः (*raviḥ*) — the Sun, रामम् (*rāmam*) — Rāma, निरीक्ष्य (*nirīkṣya*) — having seen, मुदितमनाः (*muditmanāḥ*) — one whose heart is filled with joy, निशिचरपतिसंक्षयम् (*niśicarapatisamkṣayam*) — the destruction of the king of demons, विदित्वा (*viditvā*) — having known, परमम् (*paramam*) — very much, प्रहृष्यमाणः (*prahṛṣyamāṇaḥ*) — ecstatic, त्वर (*tvara*) — hasten, इति (*iti*) — thus, वचः (*vacaḥ*) — word, अवदत् (*avadat*) — spoke.

The Sun was in the midst of the groups of gods. He saw Rāma and His heart was at once filled with joy. He could foresee the impending destruction of Rāvaṇa, the king of demons. That knowledge made Him extremely happy. He spoke only one word to Rāma: 'Hurry up'.

Suddenly one cloud moved aside and the sunlight fell upon Rāma. The Sun has showered His grace on him. In his mind, Rāma felt that it was a command from the Sun to hurry up. Rāma was very happy. This is how the prayer works. As a result of the prayer, the devotee is blessed with an inspiration, which helps him to overcome the difficulties facing him. The Sun god was also very happy, since *dharma*, in the form of Rāma, was going to vanquish the evil. The compound, *niśicarapatisaṅkṣaya* (destruction of the king of nocturnals) is very significant. When the grace of the Sun is secured, destruction of the nocturnal powers of evil is certain. The Sun, who is the eternal witness of everyone and everything in the world, responds to the prayers of the devotees without delay.

।। ओम्, शान्तिश्शान्तिश्शान्तिः, हरिः ओम्, तत्सत् ।।

। श्रीकृष्णार्पणमस्तु ।

आदित्य पञ्चविंशत्युत्तरशत नामाबलिः

Āditya Pañcaviṁśatyuttaraśata Nāmāvaliḥ

(Reverence to the Sun God with 125 Names)

ओम् रश्मिमते नमः	*Oṁ Raśmimate namaḥ*
समुद्यते नमः	*Samudyate namaḥ*
देवासुरनमस्कृताय नमः	*Devāsuranamaskṛtāya namah*
विवस्वते नमः	*Vivasvate namaḥ*
भास्कराय नमः	*Bhāskarāya namaḥ*
भुवनेश्वराय नमः	*Bhuvaneśvarāya namah*
सर्वदेवात्मकाय नमः	*Sarvadevātmakāya namaḥ*
तेजस्विने नमः	*Tejasvine namaḥ*
रश्मिभावनाय नमः	*Raśmibhāvanāya namah*
देवासुरगणलोकपालाय नमः	*Devāsuragaṇalokapālāya namaḥ*
ब्रह्मणे नमः	*Brahmaṇe namaḥ*
विष्णवे नमः	*Viṣṇave namaḥ*
शिवाय नमः	*Śivāya namaḥ*
स्कन्दाय नमः	*Skandāya namaḥ*
प्रजापतये नमः	*Prajāpataye namaḥ*
महेन्द्राय नमः	*Mahendrāya namaḥ*

धनदाय नमः	*Dhanadāya namaḥ*
कालाय नमः	*Kālāya namaḥ*
यमाय नमः	*Yamāya namaḥ*
सोमाय नमः	*Somāya namaḥ*
अपां पतये नमः	*Apāṁ Pataye namaḥ*
पितृदेवतायै नमः	*Pitṛdevatāyai namaḥ*
वसुमूर्तये नमः	*Vasumūrtaye namaḥ*
साध्यमूर्तये नमः	*Sādhyamūrtaye namaḥ*
अश्विमूर्तये नमः	*Aśvimūrtaye namaḥ*
मरुन्मूर्तये नमः	*Marunmūrtaye namaḥ*
मनवे नमः	*Manave namaḥ*
वायुमूर्तये नमः	*Vāyumūrtaye namaḥ*
वह्नये नमः	*Vahnaye namaḥ*
प्रजारूपाय नमः	*Prajārūpāya namaḥ*
प्राणाय नमः	*Prāṇāya namaḥ*
ऋतुकर्त्रे नमः	*Ṛtukartre namaḥ*
प्रभाकराय नमः	*Prabhākarāya namaḥ*
आदित्याय नमः	*Ādityāya namaḥ*
सवित्रे नमः	*Savitre namaḥ*
सूर्याय नमः	*Sūryāya namaḥ*
खगाय नमः	*Khagāya namaḥ*
पूष्णे नमः	*Pūṣṇe namaḥ*
गभस्तिमते नमः	*Gabhastimate namaḥ*
सुवर्णसदृशाय नमः	*Suvarṇasadṛśāya namaḥ*

भानवे नमः	*Bhānave namaḥ*
हिरण्यरेतसे नमः	*Hiraṇyaretase namaḥ*
दिवाकराय नमः	*Divākarāya namaḥ*
हरिदश्वाय नमः	*Haridaśvāya namaḥ*
सहस्रार्चिषे नमः	*Sahasrārciṣe namaḥ*
सप्तसप्तये नमः	*Saptasaptaye namaḥ*
मरीचिमते नमः	*Marīcimate namaḥ*
तिमिरोन्मथनाय नमः	*Timironmathanāya namaḥ*
शम्भवे नमः	*Śambhave namaḥ*
त्वष्ट्रे नमः	*Tvaṣṭre namaḥ*
मार्तण्डकाय नमः	*Mārtaṇḍakāya namaḥ*
अंशुमते नमः	*Aṁśumate namaḥ*
हिरण्यगर्भाय नमः	*Hiraṇyagarbhāya namaḥ*
शिशिराय नमः	*Śiśirāya namaḥ*
तपनाय नमः	*Tapanāya namaḥ*
अहस्कराय नमः	*Ahaskarāya namaḥ*
रवये नमः	*Ravaye namaḥ*
अग्निगर्भाय नमः	*Agnigarbhāya namaḥ*
अदितेः पुत्राय नमः	*Aditeḥ Putrāya namaḥ*
शङ्खाय नमः	*Śaṅkhāya namaḥ*
शिशिरनाशनाय नमः	*Śiśiranāśanāya namaḥ*
व्योमनाथाय नमः	*Vyomanāthāya namaḥ*
तमोभेदिने नमः	*Tamobhedine namaḥ*
ऋग्यजुस्सामपारगाय नमः	*Ṛgyajussāmapāragāya namaḥ*

घनवृष्टये नमः	*Ghanavṛṣṭaye namaḥ*
अपां मित्राय नमः	*Apāṁ Mitrāya namaḥ*
विन्ध्यवीथीप्लवङ्गमाय नमः	*Vindhyavīthīplavaṅgamāya namaḥ*
आतपिने नमः	*Ātapine namaḥ*
मण्डलिने नमः	*Maṇḍaline namaḥ*
मृत्यवे नमः	*Mṛtyave namaḥ*
पिङ्गलाय नमः	*Piṅgalāya namaḥ*
सर्वतापनाय नमः	*Sarvatāpanāya namaḥ*
कवये नमः	*Kavaye namaḥ*
विश्वस्मै नमः	*Viśvasmai namaḥ*
महातेजसे नमः	*Mahātejase namaḥ*
रक्ताय नमः	*Raktāya namaḥ*
सर्वभवोद्भवाय नमः	*Sarvabhavodbhavāya namaḥ*
नक्षत्रग्रहताराणामधिपाय नमः	*Nakṣatragrahatārāṇāmadhipāya namaḥ*
विश्वभावनाय नमः	*Viśvabhāvanāya namaḥ*
तेजसामपि तेजस्विने नमः	*Tejasāmapi Tejasvine namaḥ*
द्वादशात्मने नमः	*Dvādaśātmane namaḥ*
पूर्वाय गिरये नमः	*Pūrvāya Giraye namaḥ*
पश्चिमायाद्रये नमः	*Paścimāyādraye namaḥ*
ज्योतिर्गणानां पतये नमः	*Jyotirgaṇānāṁ Pataye namaḥ*
दिनाधिपतये नमः	*Dinādhipataye namaḥ*
जयाय नमः	*Jayāya namaḥ*

जयभद्राय नमः	*Jayabhadrāya namaḥ*
हर्यश्वाय नमः	*Haryaśvāya namaḥ*
सहस्रांशवे नमः	*Sahasrāṁśave namaḥ*
आदित्याय नमः	*Ādityāya namaḥ*
उग्राय नमः	*Ugrāya namaḥ*
वीराय नमः	*Vīrāya namaḥ*
सारङ्गाय नमः	*Sāraṅgāya namaḥ*
पद्मप्रबोधाय नमः	*Padmaprabodhāya namaḥ*
प्रचण्डाय नमः	*Pracaṇḍāya namaḥ*
ब्रह्मेशानाच्युतेशाय नमः	*Brahmeśānācyuteśāya namaḥ*
सूराय नमः	*Sūrāya namaḥ*
आदित्यवर्चसे नमः	*Ādityavarcase namaḥ*
भास्वते नमः	*Bhāsvate namaḥ*
सर्वभक्षाय नमः	*Sarvabhakṣāya namaḥ*
रौद्राय वपुषे नमः	*Raudrāya Vapuṣe namaḥ*
तमोघ्नाय नमः	*Tamoghnāya namaḥ*
हिमघ्नाय नमः	*Himaghnāya namaḥ*
शत्रुघ्नाय नमः	*Śatrughnāya namaḥ*
अमितात्मने नमः	*Amitātmane namaḥ*
कृतघ्नघ्नाय नमः	*Kṛtaghnaghnāya namaḥ*
देवाय नमः	*Devāya namaḥ*
ज्योतिषां पतये नमः	*Jyotiṣāṁ Pataye namaḥ*
तप्तचामीकराभाय नमः	*Taptacāmīkarābhāya namaḥ*
हरये नमः	*Haraye namaḥ*

विश्वकर्मणे नमः	*Viśvakarmaṇe namaḥ*
तमोऽभिनिघ्नाय नमः	*Tamo'bhinighnāya namaḥ*
रुचये नमः	*Rucaye namaḥ*
लोकसाक्षिणे नमः	*Lokasākṣiṇe namaḥ*
भूतनाशाय नमः	*Bhūtanāśāya namaḥ*
भूतस्रष्ट्रे नमः	*Bhūtasraṣṭre namaḥ*
प्रभवे नमः	*Prabhave namaḥ*
पायते नमः	*Pāyate namaḥ*
तपते नमः	*Tapate namaḥ*
वर्षते नमः	*Varṣate namaḥ*
सुप्तेषु जाग्रते नमः	*Supteṣu Jāgrate namaḥ*
भूतेषु परिनिष्ठिताय नमः	*Bhūteṣu Pariniṣṭhitāya namaḥ*
अग्निहोत्राय नमः	*Agnihotrāya namaḥ*
अग्निहोत्रिणां फलाय नमः	*Agnihotriṇāṁ Phalāya namaḥ*
परमप्रभवे नमः	*Paramaprabhave namaḥ*

Index